Bloom's

GUIDES

Alan Paton's
Cry, the Beloved Country

CURRENTLY AVAILABLE

1984
All the Pretty Horses
Beloved
Brave New World
Cry, the Beloved Country
Death of a Salesman
Hamlet
The Handmaid's Tale
The House on Mango Street
I Know Why the Caged Bird Sings
The Scarlet Letter
To Kill a Mockingbird

Bloom's
GUIDES

Alan Paton's
Cry, the Beloved Country

Edited & with an Introduction
by Harold Bloom

CHELSEA HOUSE
P U B L I S H E R S
A Haights Cross Communications Company
Philadelphia

© 2004 by Chelsea House Publishers, a subsidiary of Haights Cross
Communications.

A Haights Cross Communications ◆ Company

Introduction © 2004 by Harold Bloom.

Printed and bound in the United States of America.

First Printing
1 3 5 7 9 8 6 4 2   **3 4633 00171 7949**

Library of Congress Cataloging-in-Publication Data applied for.
ISBN: 0-7910-7572-9

Chelsea House Publishers
1974 Sproul Road, Suite 400
Broomall, PA 19008-0914

www.chelseahouse.com

Contributing editor: Neil Heims

Cover design by Takeshi Takahashi

Layout by EJB Publishing Services

Contents

Introduction

Harold Bloom

Cry, the Beloved Country (1948) is a humane Period Piece, but not at all a permanent narrative fiction. I first (and until now, last) read it when it was published, and I was eighteen. Fifty-five years later, I have gotten through it again, but only just. Its humane sentiments remain admirable, but in themselves do not constitute an aesthetic achievement.

Clearly, I prefer a decently liberal Period Piece to, say, Ayn Rand's *The Fountainhead*, a Period Piece that prophesied the emancipation of selfishness by Ronald Reagan, and the oligarchic plutocracy that the United States is metamorphosing into under George W. Bush, Cheney, Rumsfeld, Ashcroft, and their cohorts. My heart is with Alan Paton, but not my long lifetime of sustained reading of the best that has been written. It isn't so much that Paton is not Faulkner, but that he evades any authorial identity. The Hasidic rabbi Zusya observed that the Recording Angel would say to him: "Zusya, I do not ask why you were not Moses, but why did you fail to become Zusya?" The black Anglican priest, Stephen Kumalo, need not have become Desmond Tutu, but he attains no individuality of his own. Paton *assures* us that Kumalo is a spiritual guide, a Zulu hero of the devotional quest, but we are not *shown* Kumalo. At the novel's close, Kumalo is meant to represent God the Father, a rather difficult role to represent.

Religion becomes religiosity, when sentiment goes beyond an author's power of rhetoric and of mimesis. What Paton wanted to write would have been admirable, except that novels are *written-through* by Tolstoy and George Eliot, Flaubert and Faulkner, Chinua Achebe and Jose Saramago. *Cry, the Beloved Country* has wonderful intentions, but minimal characterization, and altogether unsurprising narrative development, as artless as it is benign.

Biographical Sketch

Alan Stewart Paton was born on January 11, 1903, to James Paton, a civil servant, and Eunice Warder Paton in Pietermaritzburg, Natal, in the east of South Africa. During his youth, Paton suffered physical abuse from his father which later shaped his views on corporal punishment. Also influential during his formative years was his study of literature, reading Dickens and Walter Scott, as well as his study of the Bible.

Paton graduated from Maritzburg College in 1918, and attended the University of Natal, where he graduated with distinction in physics. After his studies, Paton taught at Ixopo High School for three years. In 1928, Paton married Doris Olive Francis, at which time he returned to Pietermaritzburg and began teaching at Maritzburg College. Two years later Paton and his wife had their first son, David. Also in 1930, Paton showed his interest in race relations as he joined the South African Institute of Race Relations. In 1935 Paton left his teaching position at Maritzburg College and became principal of the Diepkloof Reformatory, a school for delinquent African boys located near Johannesburg. He held this position for thirteen years—a time period that would prove crucial to the formation of his political beliefs. A second son, Jonathan, was born in 1936, and in 1942 Paton was nominated to the Anglican Diocesan Commission, where he was to inquire into church and race relations in South Africa. During the next two years he wrote a series of articles on crime, punishment, and penal reform for *Forum*.

In 1946 Paton traveled through Europe, Canada, and America studying penal institutions—it was during this time that he began and finished his best-known work, *Cry, the Beloved Country*. Shortly after the publication of *Cry, the Beloved Country* in 1948, the National Party came into power in South Africa and instituted the practice of apartheid, a practice Paton strongly opposed. The success of the novel allowed Paton to resign from his post as principal, and in 1949 Paton attended the opening of Kurt Weill's musical adaptation of *Cry* titled

Lost in the Stars. Paton's second novel, *Too Late the Phalarope*, was published in 1953 while Paton worked at a tuberculosis settlement. Also during this time, Paton joined the Liberal Party as vice-president, and eventually became chairman in 1956. In 1954 he toured the United States to write on race relations for *Collier's*, and one year later he wrote *The Land and People of South Africa*. Paton then became trustee of the Treason Trial Defense Fund on behalf of Nelson Mandela and others. 1958 saw the publication of Paton's *Hope for South Africa* and *The People Wept*, and in 1959 he wrote his play *The Last Journey*, the story of the missionary David Livingston. After a trip to the United States in 1960, Paton's passport was confiscated by South African authorities, and in 1961 he published a collection of stories, *Tales from a Troubled Land*. Doris Olive Paton died in October 1967, two years after which he published *Kontakion*—a tribute to his departed wife. That same year, 1969, he founded the journal *Reality: A Journal of Liberal Opinion* and was remarried to Anne Margaret Hopkins. Paton continued to write, publishing *Towards the Mountain* (1980), the first volume of his autobiography, and *Ah, But Your Land Is Beautiful* (1981), his third novel. On April 12, 1988, Alan Paton died at his home in Lintrose, Botha's Hill, Natal. *Journey Continued*, the second volume of his autobiography, was published posthumously in November of that year.

The Story Behind the Story

On September 24, 1946, Alan Paton wrote to his wife from a hotel room in Trondheim, Norway: "[i]t was raining heavily & I returned to my room [from Trondheim Cathedral] & began my novel about South Africa ..."—thus beginning what would become *Cry, the Beloved Country*. Paton wrote *Cry, the Beloved Country* over the span of three months in hotel rooms as he traveled through Scandinavia, the United States, and Canada, visiting prisons and correctional facilities for delinquent boys. The last stop on his tour before returning to South Africa was San Francisco. There in the offices of the National Conference of Christians and Jews he met Aubrey and Marigold Burns. They invited him for Christmas dinner, and he showed them his manuscript, which deeply moved them. They had typewritten copies made and sent to Maxwell Perkins, the renowned editor of F. Scott Fitzgerald, Ernest Hemingway, and Thomas Wolfe, at Charles Scribner's Sons. The book was an enormous critical and popular success, worldwide. In South Africa, only the Bible outsold it. By the time of Paton's death in 1988, over fifteen million copies of the book had been sold.

Until the overwhelming success of *Cry, the Beloved Country*, Paton had worked for thirteen years as the director of Diepkloof, a reformatory for African boys. Before that he had taught at a school for well-to-do white youngsters. His contact with black youth and the success of his progressive ideas regarding prison, punishment, and reformation strongly engendered in him a growing aversion to viewing persons in terms of race and a growing opposition to imposing restrictions on racial equality and black freedom.

His own experience and his work in Diepkloof provided Paton with plot material for the novel. His egalitarian Christianity and its rootedness in love and forgiveness, and his educational theories, nurtured by advocates of freedom as a pedagogical method (such as A.S. Neill, who was practicing his ideas as headmaster of the Summerhill School in England) provided the ideological framework of the book. The social protest novels *The Grapes of Wrath*, by John Steinbeck and *Black Boy* by Richard Wright provided him with the genre. The fragmentation and shifting voices of T.S. Eliot's *The Waste Land* suggested some of the structure of the novel's narrative.

Success brought not only fame to Paton but a vivid worldwide awareness of the plight of blacks in South Africa. Soon after the book's publication, Paton resigned his position as headmaster at Diepkloof to devote himself to writing. The newly elected government soon closed that reformatory and generally instituted programs that were harsh and punitive for South African blacks.

The success of *Cry, the Beloved Country* not only propelled Paton into a successful literary career but established him as a public figure advocating the common humanity of mankind. As such he spoke throughout the world about racial equality. In South Africa, he became politically active as head of the Liberal Party, until it was declared illegal in 1968. In 1956, he was one of the founders of the Treason Trial Defense Fund (later called the Defense and Aid Fund) to support Nelson Mandela and other South African blacks opposing apartheid. The Fund was banned in 1966. In 1970, the South African regime restored Paton's passport, which it had confiscated in 1960, and he traveled again, receiving honorary degrees and teaching.

List of Characters

Stephen Kumalo is a Zulu native and an Anglican parson. His church is in Ndotsheni, a poor hillside village. After receiving a letter from Johannesburg, he sets out to find his sister and his son in the city. The novel traces his quest, his suffering, his despair, the resurrection of his faith, and his good works.

James Jarvis is a wealthy, white landowner whose farm is situated in the hills above Ndotsheni. His life and his understanding are changed after the murder of his son and his subsequent meeting with Kumalo.

Absalom Kumalo is the son of Stephen Kumalo. He panics and murders Arthur Jarvis during an attempt to rob Jarvis's house.

Arthur Jarvis is the son of James Jarvis and is murdered by Absalom Kumalo. He is an engineer by profession and a public advocate and champion of racial equality.

The Boy, Arthur Jarvis' young son, appears in the last book of *Cry, the Beloved Country* when he stops at Stephen Kumalo's church one hot afternoon. He is the instrument of the restoration of Ndotsheni after he and Stephen become friendly and he tells his grandfather of the suffering endured by the people of Kumalo's parish.

Msimangu is a Zulu Anglican priest like Kumalo. It is his letter to Kumalo which sets the plot in motion. He is an upright and virtuous man who gives Kumalo support throughout the novel and retires to monastic life after Kumalo goes back to Ndotsheni.

Father Vincent is a white Anglican priest. He too supports Kumalo throughout his quest and provides him with spiritual guidance at the time of his despair.

Mrs. Lithebe is an upright and kind black woman at whose house Kumalo stays while in Johannesburg. She provides one of the moral centers of the book.

The Director of the Reformatory supervises the reformatory for native boys where Absalom had been placed and from which he had been released when it appeared he could manage decently in the world. He helps Kumalo find his sons and he secures a lawyer for him.

John Kumalo is the brother of Stephen Kumalo and a carpenter and political organizer living in Johannesburg. He is an example of the failure of mind when heart is lacking.

Dubula, a black political organizer, is contrasted with John Kumalo. He is devoted to the good of all.

Gertrude is the sister Kumalo sets out to rescue. She went to Johannesburg with her husband, a mineworker. He abandoned both wife and child. She became a prostitute and a distiller of cheap alcohol.

The Girl is pregnant by Absalom, and nearly a child herself. She marries him after he has been sentenced to death. Kumalo takes her into his family and brings her back to Ndotsheni to live as his daughter.

Harrison is the father of Arthur Jarvis's wife. He is a bluff Englishman, not maliciously so, but racist nevertheless.

John Harrison, the son of Harrison, is a friend and admirer of Arthur Jarvis.

Napoleon Letsitsi is an agricultural demonstrator whom Jarvis brings to Ndotsheni to teach the people better farming methods.

Summary and Analysis

When the storm threatens, a man is afraid for his house....
But when the house is destroyed, there is something to
do. About a storm he can do nothing, but he can rebuild a
house.

(Cry, the Beloved Country, 108)

The Identity of Opposites

Two men search from bench to bench inside a dark and
otherwise empty church for a dry place to sit. Outside, the
downpour beats against its ill-protecting roof. One of the men,
Stephen Kumalo, the pastor of the decrepit church, is a Zulu.
The other man is James Jarvis, originally an Englishman, but
now a prosperous landowner in South Africa. Kumalo is black;
Jarvis is white. Kumalo lives in poverty on poor land, detailed
in **chapter 1**, with its "great red hills ... desolate, ... the earth ...
torn away like flesh," (4) unable to hold the rain. Jarvis is
prosperous, his land fertile:

The grass is rich and matted, you cannot see the soil. It
holds the rain and the mist, and they seep into the
ground, feeding the streams in every kloof [ravine]. (3)

The English landowner and the Zulu pastor live among the
same hills, from which "you look down on one of the fairest
valleys in Africa ... the valley of the Umzimkulu." (3) The
transformation of the hills in the descent symbolizes the
difference in the living conditions of the two men: "the rich
green hills ... grow red and bare." (3) Jarvis's territory prospers;
Kumalo's withers. Because of the racial doctrines and practices
of the South Africa of 1946—severe, yet not institutionalized
and made even worse by apartheid, as they would be in 1948,
after the election of the Afrikaner Nationalist party—Kumalo
and Jarvis, although neighbors, are nearly strangers to each
other before the events of the novel bring them together. They

seem, in fact, to be opposites. Both, however, become victims of the system and bound to each other in a brotherhood of suffering after the murder of Arthur Jarvis: Kumalo because his son is the murderer; Jarvis because it is his son who was murdered. *Cry, the Beloved Country*, through the stories of these two men, warns of the inevitable suffering that an unjust system of human relations must provoke through the harm it breeds by the way it corrupts and endangers both blacks and whites, making everyone, no matter of what color, social position, or political conviction, its victim.

Kumalo Sets Forth

After the opening chapter devoted to contrasting the contiguous hillside landscapes of Natal, *Cry, the Beloved Country* first tells Stephen Kumalo's story. It begins after he receives a letter from a fellow black Anglican priest, Msimangu, in **chapter 2**, informing him that Kumalo's sister, Gertrude, is "very sick," (7)—not saying in his letter what he will tell Kumalo later in person, that "it is not that kind of sickness," but "another, a worse kind of sickness," (23) the sickness of living in Johannesburg as a prostitute and a distiller of crude alcohol. Kumalo sets out to care for her and also to find his son, who had, at some time earlier, left their village of Ndotsheni and gone to Johannesburg in search of Gertrude. He, too, however, has been swallowed up by Johannesburg, cut off from family, tribe, tradition, and values, and Kumalo has not gotten a letter from him and has lost touch with him.

In broad, quick, yet precise strokes, Paton presents Kumalo. We first see him as he receives the letter from the child who brings it to him:

—I bring a letter, umfundisi [pastor].
—A letter, eh? Where did you get it my child?
—From the store, umfundisi. The white man asked me to bring it to you.
—That was good of you. Go well, small one. (5)

In this short dialogue, Stephen Kumalo is shown to be a man of gentle, humane, and tender spirit. The girl's shyness in front of him shows her awe and affection for him. The stylization of the language gives a formal dignity to the simplicity of his character and a solemnity to the event of receiving a letter. Its simplicity also gives fairy-tale universality to Kumalo, preparing the reader to see him as a mythic figure. Kumalo's speech, moreover, suggests intimate, tribal language, and reflects the commingling of the individual and the group, giving him a universal aspect. At the moment, he is speaking Zulu. Throughout the novel, Zulu, Afrikaans, and English itself are all represented by variously inflected English cadences. Kumalo's language, like much of the narration of the novel, is rich, too, with the resonance of biblical speech, coloring it with rectitude and moral authority.

The girl, however, does not leave:

> ... [S]he did not go at once. She rubbed one bare foot against the other, she rubbed one finger along the edge of the umfundisi's table.
> —Perhaps you might be hungry, small one.
> —Not very hungry, umfundisi.
> —Perhaps a little hungry.
> —Yes, a little hungry, umfundisi.
> —Go to the mother then. Perhaps she has some food. (5)

Kumalo is shown as a nurturer, aware that the girl stays because she is hungry—and her hunger reflects the general poverty of his village—and aware, too, of her reluctance to ask for what she wants and even to admit she is hungry. But despite his generosity, he and his wife have not much to offer besides generosity—*perhaps* there is food. Kumalo, in his role as a nurturer of the body as well as of the soul, will grow to epic stature by the end of the novel and show that the well-being of the soul and of the flesh is indivisible.

As if it were a fairy tale or a myth and thus a story common to all despite its specificity, Kumalo sets out with his wife's blessing, taking their little savings with him—money with which they planned to buy a new cooking stove and a new black suit and clean white clerical collars, for his suit is worn and his collars dingy. Even as he sets out in **chapter 3**, Kumalo is cast as a figure full of anxiety and fear. As he waits for the train, he does not attend to the landscape of the great valley below or to the sounds of the approaching train:

> There is a long way to go, and a lot of money to pay. And who knows how sick his sister may be, and what money that may cost? And if he has to bring her back, what will that cost too? And Johannesburg is a great city, with so many streets they say that a man can spend his days going up one and down another, and never the same one twice. One must catch buses too, but not as here, where the only bus that comes is the right bus.... If you take the wrong bus, you may travel to quite some other place. And they say it is dangerous to cross the street.... [T]he wife of Mpanza of Ndotsheni ... saw her son Michael killed in the street ... moved by excitement, he stepped out into the danger.... And under her eyes the great lorry crushed the life out of her son. (12)

But all these fearful thoughts culminate in "the great fear ... the greatest fear since it was so seldom spoken. Where was their son? Why did he not write anymore?" (12) At the root of all this dread is "deep down the fear of a man who lives in a world not made for him, whose own world is slipping away, dying, being destroyed, beyond any recall." (14) Kumalo, nevertheless, is not without an anchor: "The humble man reached in his pocket for his sacred book, and began to read. It was this world alone that was certain." (14)

How the sure and eternal world of the spirit as revealed in the Christian gospel meets and intervenes in the uncertain earthly world of fear and suffering is also the subject of the novel, especially of the concluding third book, and it is what gives depth of meaning to both the Kumalo and the Jarvis plot strands which Paton weaves together in the novel's first two books.

Gold and Dross

Just as the soil is the source and foundation of life for those who live on the land, and its richness or barrenness determines their prosperity, so in the great city of Johannesburg gold determines the nature of life and is at its center. The wealth of Johannesburg is built on its gold mines, and the mining of the gold depends on the pool of indigenous Africans who labor long hours in the mines for extremely poor wages. The vast pool of workers exists because the white regimes that conquered South Africa—first the British and then, more brutally, the Dutch, who became the Afrikaners—destroyed the tribal structures and cultures of the people whose land they took, and allowed for nothing to replace them but servitude. This drove the indigenous to flock to the anomic milieu of the growing city to do whatever they could to survive.

The search for his sister and his son has brought Kumalo into this historical Johannesburg in **chapter 4**, a city of exploitation, crime, and hustling. The influence of the country and the tribe has been subverted, and the connections between people, which make cooperative activity and mutual regard possible, have greatly disintegrated. Kumalo's first encounter is with a black con artist at the bus stop who fleeces him for a pound. Fortunately, Kumalo immediately afterwards approaches Mr. Mafolo, an upright Anglican businessman who leads him to the Mission House and Msimangu, one of the mainstays of support for Kumalo throughout the novel. These two encounters symbolize the two forces—betrayal and faith—which *Cry, the Beloved Country* continuously sets against each other. And they show once again Paton's technique of turning concrete details of the narrative—whether the actual hills of Ndotsheni or the careening truck which crushes Michael Mpanza before his mother's eyes (just as racism will crush the sons of Kumalo and Jarvis)—into symbolic images which serve to reiterate the novel's themes and to foreshadow future events.

By **chapter 5**, the reader knows enough to feel a premonitory shudder for Kumalo at the Mission House when in the course of a conversation he is shown a headline from the *Johannesburg Mail* that reads, "OLD COUPLE ROBBED AND BEATEN IN LONELY HOUSE. FOUR NATIVES ARRESTED." (21–22)

When they are alone, Stephen Kumalo tells Msimangu of another "great sorrow" (24) besides his sister's fall: his lost son, Absalom. Msimangu promises to help in the search for him, too. And Kumalo tells him of a brother, John Kumalo, "too busy to write," (25) who is living in Johannesburg. Msimangu knows him:

> ... [H]e is a great man of politics ... [he] has no use for the church any more. He says that what God has not done for South Africa, man must do. (25)

Exploding the finality of this argument, that man can abandon faith in God, while granting the truth of its fundamental premise, that man must act to bring justice to the world, constitutes a significant part of the drama and the tension of *Cry, the Beloved Country.* The novel postulates that the two, faith in God and the power to improve the world, are interdependent—and it is in the development of this belief that the book attains weight as a novel of ideas as well as a history of South African life.

In **chapter 6**, Msimangu takes Kumalo to Gertrude. They find her in squalor, living with her child, but abandoned by her husband, one of the numberless natives who came to Johannesburg to work in the mines. Kumalo reprimands her for the shame she has brought upon herself and upon him, and for her negligence as a mother. His reproaches move her to contrition. He takes her and the child to live in a room of the house of Mrs. Lithebe, where he is staying. He buys them clothes, and establishes the sort of bond with the child the reader expects because of the way he is with the girl who delivers the letter. It also foreshadows the important connection he establishes with Arthur's young son in the third book. Once Gertrude is settled and cared for, the search for Absalom begins. It takes Kumalo and Msimangu, his guide and confessor, through the political and economic landscapes of Johannesburg.

First Kumalo visits his brother, John, in **chapter 7**—a carpenter and a great bull of a man, who has prospered to the degree that a black man can prosper, and who sits in his shop like a tribal chief, talking politics with visitors. His analysis of the situation of blacks in South Africa is accurate, yet, what the novel shows is that it is also fatally incomplete:

—Down in Ndotsheni I am nobody.... Here in Johannesburg I am a man of some importance, of some influence. I have my own business, and when it is good, I can make ten, twelve, pounds a week....

—I do not say we are free here.... But at least I am free of the [tribal] chief... an old and ignorant man, who is nothing but a white man's dog... a trick to hold together something that the white man desires to hold together.... But it is not being held together.... It is here in Johannesburg that the new society is being built....

... I do not wish to offend you, ... but the Church too is like the chief.... A man must be faithful and meek and obedient, and he must obey the laws, whatever the laws may be....

... Here in Johannesburg ... everything is the mines. These high buildings, this wonderful City Hall, this beautiful Parktown with its beautiful houses[,] ... [t]his wonderful hospital for Europeans,... all this is built with the gold from the mines....

... Go to our hospital ... and see our people lying on the floors ... so close you cannot step over them. But it is they who dig the gold. For three shillings a day.... We live in the compounds, we must leave our wives and families behind. And when the new gold is found, it is not we who will get more for our labor. It is the white man's shares that will rise.... They do not think, here is a chance to pay more for our labor... only, here is a chance to build a bigger house and buy a bigger car....

... [I]t is built on our backs, on our sweat, on our labor. (35–37)

This is all true and eloquently expressed. It is the meaning a careless reader who reads *Cry, the Beloved Country* as a protest novel, might take away from the book, but John Kumalo presents only an analysis of the problem, not a resolution. It is, moreover, an analysis spoken by a man whom Paton portrays in the book as worse than cynical. He is selfish, power hungry, cowardly, without loyalty, and corrupt. John Kumalo, for example, although living close to Gertrude, who is his sister, too, did not devote himself to rescuing her from her life of vice and degradation. When Stephen speaks of her, John can only make excuses, placing the blame for his failure on Gertrude: "I myself tried to persuade her, but she did not agree, so we did not meet anymore," and speaking with the detachment of a sociologist: "Johannesburg is not a place for a woman alone." (38) But, of course, she would not have been alone had he cared for her like a brother. *Cry, the Beloved Country*, as its title indicates, is a novel of tears, not of anger, of feeling as well as of thought, because it is a novel not of protest but of reconciliation. It is not through anger, or self-assertion, the book says, but through mercy, reconciliation, and recognition of the needs of others, through selfless love, that progress is made and justice accomplished. For reconciliation to be possible, according to Paton, faith in the divine, transcendent and merciful nature of a Godhead—Jesus, for him—is necessary, for it is that faith in the good which is eternal which enables the humanity of the present.

In the street, after Kumalo and Msimangu have left John Kumalo, Msimangu considers the argument they have just heard, and voices the bedrock doctrine as well as the abiding fear of the novel. "Many of the things he said are true," Msimangu says. He continues, however, and shows the flaw in John Kumalo's world view:

Because the white man has power, we too want power.... But when a black man gets power, when he gets money, he is a great man if he is not corrupted. I have seen it often. He seeks power and money to put right what is wrong, and when he gets them, why, he enjoys the power and money.... Some of us think when we have power, we shall revenge ourselves ... and because this desire is corrupt, we are corrupted, and the power has no heart in it....

... But there is only one thing that has power completely, and that is love. Because when a man loves, he seeks no power, and therefore he has power. I see only one hope for our country, and that is when white men and black men, desiring neither power nor money, but desiring only the good of their country, come together and work for it.

... I have only one fear in my heart, that one day when they are turned to loving, they will find we are turned to hating. (39–40)

Journey into Fear

From John Kumalo, Stephen and Msimangu have learned that Absalom was friendly with John's son Matthew, who left his father's home because—John Kumalo explains to his brother and Msimangu in words tellingly similar to those he offered to excuse himself for not having exercised his responsibility for his sister, Gertrude—he [Matthew Kumalo] "did not agree well with his second mother," (38) and he [John] couldn't reconcile them. He says that both Matthew and Absalom went to work in a textiles factory. At the textiles factory, Kumalo and Msimangu learn that Absalom has not worked there for a year, but they learn also that he may be staying at the house of Mrs. Ndlela. When they visit her they learn he is no longer there, but there is a forwarding address. In a word he manages to exchange with Mrs. Ndlela out of Kumalo's hearing, Msimangu learns that Absalom left because both she and her husband disapproved of his friends.

Getting to Mrs. Mkize's house in **chapter 8**, the next stop on their journey to find Absalom, takes them into the midst of a political struggle. Kumalo and Msimangu must travel some eleven miles from the center to an outlying neighborhood of Johannesburg. But there is a bus boycott by mine workers protesting a fare increase. Instead of riding the bus, the mine workers spend some six hours of their long workday walking to and from the mines. And they ask all others who usually ride the bus to support them in the boycott by also refraining from using the buses. Paton does not merely use this incident for local color or historical verisimilitude or even to make a political point—although the entire novel does repeatedly serve as an indictment of South African racism. He weaves into the one fabric of the novel many threads, and reproduces the wholeness of a world fashioned by the racism which defined everything in the South Africa of which he writes. The background not only enriches the story of the novel, but serves to illuminate the dispositions of its characters through their responses, and keeps the themes of the novel in the forefront of reader awareness.

As they plan to board the bus, Kumalo and Msimangu are stopped by Dubula, a black political organizer who is leading the boycott. Dubula is a character Paton sets in contrast to John Kumalo. Both believe in political action against racial injustice, and both have left the Church and regard it as an insufficient instrument in the struggle against racial oppression. John Kumalo, however, as seen, is portrayed as self-interested, power-seeking, and unwilling to risk his own security or comfort in the pursuit of his beliefs; nor does he care about the good of others. Msimangu says of him that he has a voice, but no heart. Dubula, on the other hand, is shown as authentically committed to political change and the popular welfare with all his heart. His concern is with the common good, not his own aggrandizement. In him Paton shows the unity of individual and social interest. In John Kumalo he shows the cynical exploitation of social advancement as a means of achieving only self-advancement and self-centered gratification, even at the expense of others, as is made clear in Book II. Dubula is upright and near to Stephen Kumalo in spirit despite his distance from Christian belief. Both dedicate themselves to the good of others. The depth of this devotion and self-transcendence in Stephen Kumalo transforms him into an agent of divine benevolence in the midst of human malevolence, as the third book of *Cry, the Beloved Country* shows.

After Dubula explains the bus boycott to them, the hardship of the miner's struggle and the economic consequences of the fare increase, Stephen and Msimangu begin the eleven-mile walk to Mrs. Mkize's. It is on this journey that one of the sublime incidents of the novel occurs. It not only shows another aspect of black-white relations in South Africa, but it gives to the later narration of Arthur Jarvis's work and of his father's enlightenment a foundation in reality. And it is a proof that Arthur Jarvis's utopian vision is not hopelessly unrealistic. Shortly after Kumalo and Msimangu set out on their long walk, a car driven by a white man stops, and the man offers to give them a lift, which they gratefully accept. When he lets them off at their destination, they are astonished to see that he does not continue in the same direction but turns around. He had not actually been going in their direction but was deliberately aiding them, one of the many among the whites who were actively supporting the black mine workers in their boycott, despite police harassment.

At Mrs. Mkize's there is the first sign that Absalom may be in serious trouble. Mrs. Mkize herself is an unfriendly woman, reluctant to give any information about Absalom except that he has not lived in her house for over a year. But her eyes speak:

—How did he behave himself, this young man Absalom, Kumalo asked her?
Have no doubt it is fear in her eyes. Have no doubt it is fear now in his eyes also. It is fear, here in this house.
—I saw nothing wrong, she said.
—But you guessed something was wrong.
—There was nothing wrong, she said.
—Then why are you afraid?
—I am not afraid, she said.
—Then why do you tremble? asked Msimangu. (46–47)

In addition to providing information which advances the plot, this exchange suggests there is a wordless, sensory connection between people, and thus that mankind participates collectively in a common being and functions through a common intelligence as well as individually. This is a connection racism attempts to repudiate, but it cannot be destroyed, only subverted and made the source of pain and ill. Its reality serves as the foundation of Paton's Christian humanism and the lesson of Book III of *Cry, the Beloved Country*.

In the street, Kumalo tells Msimangu he fears something is wrong, and Msimangu returns to Mrs. Mkize by himself. After his threats to call the police and his oaths on the Bible that he is not looking for information to use against her, he learns from her that Absalom and his friends had brought stolen goods to her house and sorted them there. He learns further that Absalom had been seen with Hlabeni, a taxi driver in the neighborhood. They find Hlabeni, who also shows fear when asked about Absalom, but after being assured that they do not seek trouble, but only want to find the boy, he informs them that he heard Absalom had gone to Shantytown to live among the squatters there.

Once again in a section **(chapter 9)** describing the difficulty blacks have in finding a place to live—the squalor of the housing available, the political organizing required because of these conditions, and even the makeshift communities that form despite everything—personal and social narratives converge, and Paton shows the soil that spawns the kind of life Absalom Kumalo has come to live. Not only Absalom: Paton weaves into his story vignettes of life and culture among the Africans, whose customs have been torn from their culture like the richness from the soil in the hills of Ndotsheni. Besides showing the violations of humanity, however, he also shows the steadfast grounding in tradition among many of the native people. They are the ones who have kept the strength and dignity of their traditional culture. Often it is because of their full-souled devotion to the Christian gospel, which ironically, they got from the Europeans in exchange for their land. Among those who embody steadfast virtue in the midst of the racial oppression is Mrs. Lithebe, the generous woman who allows Stephen Kumalo to board in her house while in Johannesburg. Paton reintroduces Mrs. Lithebe in **chapter 10**, when Kumalo brings his sister Gertrude and Gertrude's child to stay at her house, and later also brings Stephen's pregnant girlfriend to stay with her. Kumalo and Msimangu respectfully call Mrs. Lithebe Mother, and she does represent the generous devotion and willingness to help that the figure of a mother is used ideally to represent. She reprimands Gertrude for her loose companions and she rebukes Gertrude and the girl for idle chatter and foolish laughing. And as she does, she also serves as a choral reinforcement for the reader's perception of Kumalo's nobility: "This old man has been hurt greatly," she tells them, "and he shall not be hurt any more, not in my house." (120)

When praised for her aid, she always responds with a rhetorical question: Why else were people born but to do kindness? This is perhaps the fundamental premise of the novel itself.

Finding Absalom Lost

In Shantytown, Kumalo and Msimangu discover that Absalom no longer lives there. Mrs. Hlatshwayos tells them:

—He stayed with me, umfundisi. We took pity on him because he had no place to go. But I am sorry to tell you that they took him away, and I heard that the magistrate had sent him to the reformatory. (64)

The reformatory that Absalom is sent to is modeled on the one in Diepkloof of which Paton was still the director at the time of writing *Cry, the Beloved Country*. (In fact he wrote the book during his tour through Scandinavia and North America to observe the way reformatories were run in those lands.) Like Paton's, the reformatory Absalom was sent to was run on non-punitive principles, dedicated to the idea that freedom and trust, not punishment and constraint, are corrective. Kumalo and Msimangu learn from the director of the reformatory that it was only a month before that Absalom was released:

We made an exception in his case, partly because of his good behavior, partly because of his age, but mainly because there was a girl who was pregnant by him. She came here to see him, and he seemed fond of her, and anxious about the child that would be born. And the girl too seemed fond of him, so with all these things in mind, and with his solemn undertaking that he would work for his child and its mother, we asked the Minister to let him go.... [E]verything is arranged for the marriage. This girl has no people, and your son told us he had no people, so I myself and my native assistant have arranged it. (66)

The director drives them to Pimville, where Absalom is working in a factory and living with his girl. Their hopes of finding him are quickly dashed, however, when they learn from the girl that Absalom has not been home for days. From the factory head they learn that he has been absent from work, too. Msimangu is bitter at the wayward behavior of his people. The director is angry at his failure with Absalom. Kumalo, grieving and suffering, nevertheless, thinks of his own obligation to the girl and to the child she is carrying. He reminds Msimangu, when Msimangu tells him he can do nothing, that "[t]he child will be my grandchild." (68) The director of the reformatory leaves them with the reassurance that he will continue to search for Absalom. Perhaps, he offers, the boy has been injured and taken to the hospital. Msimangu suggests that Kumalo rest for a few days and go with him to Ezenzeleni, where Msimangu will hold a service for a congregation of blind people.

The evening before they set out for Ezenzeleni, Kumalo and Msimangu are spending a "pleasant evening" (71) at the Mission House with Father Vincent, a white priest, in **chapter 11**. Kumalo is telling them about Ndotsheni, and Father Vincent is describing the English countryside and Westminster Abbey. Their pastoral ease is disturbed, and Kumalo's anxious premonitions are recalled, when another priest brings in the *Evening Star* with its terrible headline: "MURDER IN PARKWOLD. WELL-KNOWN CITY ENGINEER SHOT DEAD. ASSAILANTS THOUGHT TO BE NATIVES."

(72) This is the announcement, although he only senses it as yet, which brings to a culmination Kumalo's search for his son.

In the way that *Cry, the Beloved Country* ties together personal and political fortune as a revolving series of causes and effects, this announcement with its entirely personal significance for Kumalo is brought to him through the most public of channels, the newspaper. It is by the newspaper, too, that the reader is first introduced to Arthur Jarvis, son of James Jarvis, the white man we encountered sheltering in the leaky church with Kumalo. This public introduction is fitting, for Arthur Jarvis was a public man, a husband, father, and an engineer, yes, but just as significantly, an activist writer and speaker working for racial justice and social equality. The news story reports that a manuscript he must have been working on at the time of his murder was found on his bedside table, "The Truth about Native Crime," an essay analyzing the social causes of presumably individual behavior.

"Perhaps you might have known him," Father Vincent says to Stephen Kumalo. "It says that he was the only child of Mr. James Jarvis, of High Place, Carisbrooke." Kumalo responds, "sorrowfully,"

> —I know the father.... I mean I know him well by sight and name, but we have never spoken.... [H]e sometimes rode past our church. But I did not know the son ... yet I remember there was a small bright boy, and he too sometimes rode on his horse past our church. A small bright boy.... (72)

But later to Msimangu, Kumalo confides:

> —This thing .... This thing. Here in my heart there is nothing but fear. Fear, fear, fear.
> —I understand. Yet it is foolishness to fear that one thing in this great city, with its thousands and thousands of people.
> —It is not a question of wisdom and foolishness. It is just fear. (74)

It is not only Stephen Kumalo who is fearful. Paton asserts that the racist system brings fear to everyone, and once again the narrative structure of *Cry, the Beloved Country* shows the intersection of the personal and the social. In a series of vignettes following the news of Arthur Jarvis's murder, he shows how waves of fear roll through all segments of Johannesburg society. In these vignettes, too, he shows the varieties of political responses to what is defined as the problem of black crime, from calls for tougher action, stricter policing, and complete racial separation to attempts to find social causes and humane responses. Paton ends this section in **chapter 12**, however, not with a proposal but with a lamentation, as if suggesting that before there can be any serious thought given to the matter there must be a deeper, personal and collective, emotional response that helps to cleanse the soul of the pervasive hurt that the system of racism inflicts:

> Cry, the beloved country for the unborn child that is the inheritor of fear. Let him not love the earth too deeply. Let him not laugh too gladly when the water runs through his fingers, nor stand too silent when the setting sun makes red the veld with fire. Let him not be too moved when the birds of his land are singing, nor give too much of his heart to a mountain or a valley. For fear will rob him of all if he gives too much. (80)

After the cadenza on social fear and the panic response to the slaying of Arthur Jarvis, Paton returns in a series of staccato episodes to the Kumalo plot and shifts from the great social fear to the great fear of one man. Kumalo knows that Absalom is wanted by the police but does not know why, and is haunted by the fear that it is for the murder of Arthur Jarvis. Between the period of his fear of the possibility and the time that he finds out it is so, Kumalo suffers hopelessness and a crisis of faith. He tells Msimangu: "There is no prayer left in me. I am dumb here inside. I have no words at all." After they bid good night to each other, the narrator observes, "There are times, no doubt, when God seems no more to be about the world." (74)

During the time of suspense, Kumalo finds comfort hearing Msimangu preaching in Ezenzeleni in **chapter 13**, especially when he quotes this passage of the Christian gospel:

> Even the youths shall faint and be weary
> and the young men shall utterly fall.
> but they that wait upon the Lord
> shall renew their strength,
> they shall mount up with wings as eagles,
> they shall run and not be weary
> and they shall walk and not faint. (91–92)

But it is only a partial comfort, and when he learns that Absalom is the murderer of Arthur Jarvis it is no comfort at all. The introduction of this biblical passage is one of those instances of foreshadowing that Paton practices throughout the novel, now not for the sake of plot *per se* but to prepare the reader for the metaphysics of the final book, where both fathers, Kumalo and Jarvis, will be actors in a parable demonstrating that those who "wait upon the Lord" do experience renewed strength, even if it is mingled with great suffering and grief, and are able to "walk and not faint," which means to accomplish the things which must be accomplished.

Absalom's arrest and confession bring forth great despair in his father, and that despair is mixed with anger at the boy which he expresses in his reprimands when he visits him in prison in **chapter 14**. The reprimands are undoubtedly "correct," but they interfere with the boy's ability to make contact with his father, making him only withdraw into himself, and they keep Kumalo from the real experience of his bottomless grief. Similarly, the young white director of the reformatory, the figure modeled upon Paton, shows a cold anger and bitter disappointment at the failure of his work. He snaps when Stephen looks to him to know whether he ought to get a lawyer for Absalom, saying, "It is not my work to get lawyers.... It is my work to reform...." (102) This, too, is undoubtedly a fair response, but it prevents him from expressing the bond of grief that he shares with Kumalo. Later, in a scene with Kumalo which again suggests the philosophy of the third section of the book, the young director reconciles himself emotionally with Kumalo, explaining:

> I am sorry, umfundisi, that I spoke such angry words.... I spoke like that because I was grieved and because I try to give myself to my work. And when my work goes wrong, I hurt myself and I hurt others also. But then I grow ashamed, and that is why I am here. (105)

His confession exemplifies the spirit of *Cry, the Beloved Country*, for the philosophy of the book is that in order to overcome human troubles, psychological understanding and transcendental values are far more important than rebuke and penalization.

Arrested along with Absalom—when the police found him, he made a voluntary and full confession—were his cousin, Matthew (John Kumalo's son), and another young man, Johannes Pafuri. After Kumalo and his brother visit their sons in prison, the novel's great theme of betrayal is introduced. John Kumalo's strategy is for his son to lie and say he did not participate in the attempted robbery and murder, that he wasn't even there, and to say that Absalom is lying. This recourse underscores not only his baseness but the emptiness of his liberation politics; he demonstrates his inability to deal justly, his lack of a loyal heart, and his contempt for solidarity with the suffering of others. He is willing to sacrifice his nephew and his own brother in the pursuit of his own interest. Unlike the director of the reformatory, he has no shame. Indeed, the director of the reformatory, as they are leaving, and after he has heard John Kumalo explain why he is taking a lawyer for his son—"You see, my brother, there is no proof that my son or this other young man was there at all.... Who will believe your son?"—says to him, "You are a clever man, but thank God you are not my brother." (101–102) Unlike Msimangu, the director of the reformatory, or Stephen Kumalo, John Kumalo has no shame. He is set up as representing the way one must not be.

It is a disposition entirely opposite to John Kumalo's that

Father Vincent instructs Kumalo to cultivate in **chapter 15**. Kumalo's grief at the murder is mixed with anger at his son. Absalom is penitent only because as he is afraid for himself, not because he is ashamed of his deed or in pain for the grief he has brought to others. This failing in Absalom compounds his father's sense of abandonment. He is shut in with anger against his son rather than able to extend himself to the lost boy.

—He is a stranger.... I cannot touch him, I cannot reach him. I see no shame in him, no pity for those he has hurt. Tears come to his eyes, but it seems to me he weeps only for himself, not for his wickedness, but for his danger.... Can a person lose all sense of evil? A boy brought up as he was brought up? I see only his pity for himself, he who has made two children fatherless. I tell you, that whosoever offends one of these little ones, it were better....

—Stop, cried Father Vincent. You are beside yourself. Go and pray, go and rest. And do not judge your son too quickly. He too is shocked into silence, maybe.

Kumalo stood up. I trust that is so, he said, but I have no hope anymore. What did you say I must do? Yes, pray and rest.

There was no mockery in his voice, and Father Vincent knew that it was not in this man's nature to speak mockingly. But so mocking were the words that the white priest caught him by the arm, and said to him urgently, sit down, I must speak to you as a priest.... I said pray and rest. Even if it is only words that you pray.... And do not pray for yourself, and do not pray to understand the ways of God.... And why you go on, when it would seem better to die, that is a secret. Pray for Gertrude, and for her child, and for the girl that is to be your son's wife, and for the child that will be your grandchild. Pray for your wife and all at Ndotsheni. Pray for the woman and the children that are bereaved. Pray for the soul of him who was killed.... And do not fear to pray for your son, and for his amendment.

—And give thanks where you can give thanks. For nothing is better.

... When Kumalo would have thanked him, he said, we do what is in us, and why it is in us, that is also a secret. It is Christ in us, crying that men may be succoured and forgiven, even when He Himself is forsaken.

—I shall pray for you, [Father Vincent concluded], night and day. That I shall do and anything more that you ask. (110)

This passage is central to the entire novel. It defines *Cry, the Beloved Country* as devotional literature. Its purpose is to praise God and to show how to praise God and how to avoid despair. It is in light of this passage that the novel must be read, especially the last book. It is saying that God fulfills His purposes in the actions of men when men act in accordance with their faith in God's goodness rather than in despair at God's absence—when they allow the Christ in them to work—for the degree of God's absence or presence is measured by the acts of individual men. And as *Cry, the Beloved Country* is a didactic book, Father Vincent's sermon also establishes the essential text for which the fable of the novel is the *exemplum*: let the care of each of us be not for his or her self but for the other, and we ourselves will find ourselves cared for. Thus it marks the initiation of the final phase in Kumalo's journey, his ordination as the agent of God's grace and the recipient of that grace. The force of grace and the efficacy of prayer are demonstrated in the next development of the plot.

The day after his meeting with Father Vincent, Kumalo goes back to Pimville in **chapter 16** to see the girl whom Absalom is to marry. He tells her of the murder and that he has arranged for Absalom to marry her before his imprisonment and probable execution, if she wishes it. She does. He also tells her he will care for her as his daughter and her child-to-be as his grandchild. He asks if it is agreeable to her to go back to Ndotsheni with him. She tells him very much so. The brilliance of his goodness to her—young as she is, she has already been betrayed and abandoned by many men—brings joy to her and fixes in her a sense of gratitude, love, and devotion, and brings home the truth of Father Vincent's teaching. Kumalo understands his interaction with the girl in the light of Father Vincent's prayers:

> When he turned back to look at her, she was smiling at him. He walked on like a man from whom a pain has been lifted a little, not altogether, but a little.... And he remembered too, with a sudden and devastating shock, that Father Vincent had said, I shall pray night and day. At the corner he turned, and looking back, saw that the girl was still watching him. (116)

God's grace which descends upon him in response to Father Vincent's prayers comes in the form of the girl's love and is the result of his own goodness.

The Father as the Fulfillment of the Son

In Book II, the Kumalo plot recedes and the background of the first book, the story of Arthur Jarvis, comes to the foreground. The story is told by exploring the effect his life and thought have on his bereaved father. Arthur is resurrected in his father when his father begins to act according to his son's values and vision.

The second book of *Cry, the Beloved Country* begins at **chapter 18** with the same words that open the first book, emphasizing the connection between the white farmer and the black pastor despite the social attempt to alienate them from each other. Instead, however, of directing us to Kumalo's poor parish the reader is taken to the High Place, where Jarvis's farm is situated. From there one can survey everything below. The erosion that is impoverishing the people and the countryside of the lower region is creeping up the hillsides and threatening the white citadels as well as the black enclaves. Making matters worse, it is a time of drought. Drought also serves as metaphor for the social reality of South Africa. It is a time of spiritual dryness. There is a social restriction on the flow of human sympathy between blacks and whites. The social erosion, the erosion of the human sense of the humanity of others, is, therefore, also severe.

From the heights from which James Jarvis surveys the land below, he sees a car driving up the road to him. It brings the news of his son's murder and the beginning of his journey, which parallels Kumalo's. He sets off with his wife for Johannesburg. He will go to his son's funeral, visit the house Arthur lived in and especially his study, and attend Absalom's trial and have his first encounter with Stephen Kumalo.

Just as the first book of *Cry, the Beloved Country* presentes the picture of black life in South Africa, so in the second book, Paton presents a cross section of white, English (rather than Dutch or Afrikaner) South African society. The conversations between James Jarvis and Harrison (Arthur's wife's father), and Harrison's son John reflect the detached liberal racism of the older generation in **chapters 19–21**. "I try to treat a native decently, but he's not my food and drink," Harrison tells Jarvis. "And to tell you the truth, these crimes [like the murder of Arthur Jarvis] put me off." (140) Later he says:

> God knows what's coming to the country, I don't. I'm not a nigger-hater, Jarvis. I try to give 'em a square deal, decent wages, and a clean room, and reasonable time off. Our servants stay with us for years. But the natives as a whole are getting out of hand. (150)

In these conversations with Harrison and his son, at Arthur's funeral, in Arthur's study, when he reads the unfinished essay Arthur was writing moments before he was killed, Jarvis learns for the first time fully what kind of man his son was.

The church where Arthur's funeral takes place "had been too small for all who wanted to come." And it was full of people of all races.

> White people, black people, coloured people, Indians—it was the first time that Jarvis and his wife had sat in a

church with people who were not white.... People that he did not know shook hands with him ... speaking simply of his son. The black people—yes, the black people also—it was the first time he had ever shaken hands with black people. (148)

The funeral marks the beginning of Jarvis' illumination. The loss of his son is the precipitating experience that increases his own humanity. Hearing Harrison and his son John speak of Arthur, he gets a sense of Arthur's character and his influence on other people. Perhaps the best example of Arthur's integrity comes in the following anecdote Harrison tells Jarvis:

> ... [Arthur] was hot about the native compound system in the Mines, and wanted the Chamber to come out one hundred percent for settled labour ... wife and family to come with the man.... Hathaway of the Chamber of the Mines spoke to me about it.... Asked me if I wouldn't warn the lad to pipe down a bit, because his firm did a lot of business with the Mines. So I spoke to him, told him I knew he felt deeply about these things, but asked him to go slow a bit. Told him there was Mary [Arthur's wife] to consider, and the children.
>   —I've spoken to Mary, he said to me. She and I agree that it's more important to speak the truth than to make money.... My son John was there, [Harrison] said, looking at Arthur as though he were God Almighty.... I asked [Arthur] ... about his partners. After all their job was to sell machinery to the Mines. I've discussed it with my partners, he said to me, and if there's any trouble, I've told them I'll get out. And what would you do? I asked him. What won't I do? he said. (140)

It is in Arthur's study, however, that Jarvis gains a real understanding of who his son was and what he stood for. Cases of books line the walls. Between the books are hung several images: Abraham Lincoln, of the crucified Christ and a leafless willow by a river in winter. The desk is strewn with invitations to speak to numerous organizations. All these things, actual in themselves, also have symbolic value, representing aspects of Arthur, his life, and his influences. The winter tree suggests the current state of South Africa, barren and cold because of its racism, but still austerely beautiful and ready for a change of season. Lincoln represents the political aspect of the struggle against racial injustice, and the crucifixion scene represents the spiritual discipline and the sacrifice essential for any dedication to making goodness prevail. It implies acceptance of suffering as necessary for purgation, resurrection, and renewal.

On Arthur's table, too, is the draft of the essay he was writing when the disturbance in the kitchen called him away and to his death. Jarvis reads the essay several times, and Paton shows the reader the essay as he reads it, so that Arthur appears in *Cry, the Beloved Country* as a memory, as an intelligence, and as a guide for future action. He combines the several elements we see distributed among the various political reformers in the book: intelligence, heart, devotion, and a readiness to sacrifice. Kumalo—who had seen him riding his red horse through Ndotsheni as a boy—says of him in words which will reverberate in the last book that "there was a brightness in him." (181)

In Book II as in Book I, Paton weaves the social context into the story: while Absalom's trial is going on (**chapters 22–28**), a new and rich vein of gold is discovered, and Paton presents the social forces stirred by the discovery, focusing on the tension between the Afrikaner owners of the mines and the native laborers who work the mines and on the conflicting demands on the wealth thus introduced. The discovery of the gold culminates in a strike by the mine workers. One of the agitators for the workers is John Kumalo. As is usual in Paton's depiction of John Kumalo, much of what he says in his powerful public speeches is valid, but coming from his mouth it is inauthentic and self-serving. Paton emphasizes once again that it is the spirit behind the word, which derives from the actions of the man, which gives the word meaning.

The climax of the second book is not Absalom's trial and

conviction but the first encounter between Kumalo and Jarvis while the trial is going on in **chapter 25**.

When he was leaving Ndotsheni on his journey to Johannesburg to begin his search, one of his neighbors asked Kumalo if he could find out where his daughter was. Dutifully, Kumalo visits the house of the girl's last known employer, who happens to be the niece of James Jarvis's wife, and the day Kumalo comes to make enquiry, Jarvis happens to be there. When Kumalo sees him he is taken by great fear. Jarvis, for his part, recognizes Kumalo as the parson of Ndotsheni, but does not know that he is the father of the boy who killed his son:

> —I know you, umfundisi, [Jarvis] said.
> The suffering in the old man's face smote him.... Jarvis said to him, not looking at him, there is something between you and me, but I do not know what it is.... You are in fear of me. But I do not know what it is. You need not be in fear of me....
> —It is very heavy, umnumzana. It is the heaviest thing of all my years.
> He lifted his face, and there was in it suffering that Jarvis had not seen before. Tell me, he said, it will lighten you.
> —I am afraid, umnumzana.
> —I see you are afraid.... It is that which I do not understand.... [Y]ou need not be afraid. I shall not be angry. There will be no anger in me against you.
> —Then, said the old man, this thing that is the heaviest thing of all my years, is the heaviest thing of all your years also.
> Jarvis looked at him, at first bewildered, but then something came to him. You can only mean one thing, he said, you can only mean one thing. But I still do not understand.
> —It was my son that killed your son, said the old man.
> (180)

The sympathy between the two men is visceral, immediate, and profound. They speak to each other in simple words, yet their words are charged with the fullness of their own experience and their deep sympathy for and acknowledgement of each other. They speak the language of the heart and of relationship, and it is their connection that Paton presents as the solution to the racial problem: each embracing the other's suffering as his own. "My heart," Kumalo tells Jarvis, "holds a deep sorrow for you, and for the inkosikazi [Jarvis's wife] and for the young inkosikazi [Arthur's wife], and for the children." (181) When Kumalo leaves, Jarvis follows him to the gate. They wish each other well at parting, and Jarvis stands watching until Kumalo is out of sight. The formality of their language, the artificiality which removes it from commonplace utterance and sanctifies it, serves to convey the intensity and sublimity of the experience of their meeting and of their exchange. Their speech shows an authenticity that John Kumalo's, for example, is entirely without. And for Paton, as the third book of *Cry, the Beloved Country* shows, the authentic recognition of one person by another, often achieved through the recognition of the other's suffering, is the basis for a society of brotherhood.

In **chapter 28**, Absalom's trial results in a guilty verdict for him and the sentence of death by hanging. It results in a dismissal of the charges for lack of evidence against Matthew Kumalo and Johannes Pafuri. Their victory was achieved at Absalom's expense. They are lying, but their lawyer shapes their case to undermine Absalom's credibility. John Kumalo's turpitude also results in a break between Stephen and John Kumalo, who throws Stephen out of his store and locks the door after him when Stephen shows him the face of his betrayal

.

The Government of Love

The ostensible story of *Cry, the Beloved Country* is essentially concluded with the end of the second book in **chapter 29**. A mellower man than before, and with broader human sympathies, Jarvis lives with his son's death and the melancholy awareness of knowing his son better in death than in life. His spirit, also, has been touched by his son, and when he leaves Johannesburg, he gives Arthur's friend John Harrison an envelope to be opened after his train has gone. It contains a check for a thousand pounds to be given to the African Boys' Club which Arthur had been supporting. Tried and strengthened in his humanity, Kumalo returns to Ndotsheni without his son—who is in Pretoria awaiting execution but hoping for unlikely executive clemency and a life sentence. His sister, Gertrude, also is not with him. She had been portrayed as a light woman, more prone to amusement than virtue, but capable of amendment and religious feeling. On the morning of the return to Ndotsheni, however, she is not in her room. Apparently she has returned to the netherworld of Johannesburg. Kumalo hears no more of her. The two whom Kumalo went to retrieve, he could not. But he brings home with him his sister's son and his son's pregnant wife, rescuing them from the alienation and brutality of the city. His endurance and forbearance in quest and in suffering are rewarded, certainly, by the esteem and the love of all those around him. And his friend Msimangu, who is going to withdraw from the world and enter a monastery, gives him his own savings, and Kumalo returns home with money enough to buy himself new clerical garments and his wife a new stove. Yet he still bears the burden of suffering. And returning to Ndotsheni brings him once again to a world of suffering. The injustice of South Africa will continue to exist and undoubtedly will be the context for many more stories of suffering, defeat, endurance, and redemption. But there is a third book to the novel.

The misery of Johannesburg is social and man-made, the result of racism, economic injustice, exploitation, poverty, greed, and self-centeredness—awful in themselves, but easily remedied, if there were in mankind a change of heart. But that change of heart and its accompanying change of mind will not come without an alteration in the spirit to a spirit of love, and in the ability of people to follow the government of love. In the third book of *Cry, the Beloved Country*, Paton transforms the novel from a book about the social evil of racism—and its eruption in one crime—to an anatomy of transcendent power and to a visionary, pastoral romance in which the sympathy of men for each other and the interplay of man and nature accomplish the will of God.

The situation to which Kumalo returns in Ndotsheni in **Book III** is in many ways like the one Oedipus comes upon in Thebes: "... the soil is sick almost beyond healing.... [T]he rains will not fall; [the people] cannot plow or plant, and there will be hunger in this valley." (219) Kumalo himself becomes a figure like Oedipus. He is like the figure of Oedipus as he is portrayed at the beginning of *Oedipus the King*, the man of practical solutions and insight who must bring succor to his people who are dying because of the plague that is withering the land, and he is also like Oedipus as he is presented in *Oedipus at Colonus* after his blinding enlightenment, when he has become a holy man because of his suffering and his very presence therefore has power to influence supernatural things. Kumalo is, after all, both a man who has been tested with affliction and a priest, and as such a representative of the sacred and a channel to the sacred. He has within him both practical wisdom and a saintly disposition.

Upon his return in **chapter 30**, Kumalo is greeted with gladness by his congregation, and then, as the people of Thebes supplicated Oedipus, these complain to him: "It is dry here, umfundisi. We cry for rain.... It is known to [God] alone what we shall eat." (221) As they walk, they go by a path that

goes by the little stream that runs by the church. Kumalo stops to listen to it, but there is nothing to hear.
—The stream does not run, my friend.
—It has been dry for a month, umfundisi. (221)

The plague that is sickening the land, like the plague in *Oedipus the King*, is the result of a crime, here of fratricide rather than patricide, although the crime of the son nearly kills his father and the father of his victim. Reciprocally, the crimes of the society of the fathers (racial injustice and the contempt for persons which it generates) have bred the conditions for the crimes of the sons. It is the larger crime of racial injustice and inhumanity, of contempt for brotherhood emblematized by the fratricidal crime of the plot, that the novel now addresses in the sickness of the land. It is as if a homeopathic magic were at work; the criminal disease in mankind manifests itself in Nature. For Nature to be whole, the corruption in mankind must be undone. When the spirit has been violated and the consequences made manifest, another act of remediation reaffirming the holiness of the spirit is necessary to undo the harm wrought on nature by the violation. Kumalo, in his priestly role recognizes this:

> Kumalo began to pray regularly in his church for the restoration of Ndotsheni. But he knew that was not enough. Somewhere down here on earth men must come together, think something, do something. (229)

And because of the fineness and gentleness of his spirit, and the devotion of James Jarvis to the memory of his son, and because of the innocent goodness of uncorrupted youth, he accomplishes it.

Kumalo sets out in **chapter 31**, first to talk with the chief, the titular head of the broken Zulu tribe in Ndotsheni, a man with great pride and no power. Their interview produces nothing but the chief's impatience and annoyance at being reminded of problems he is incapable of handling, and he offers words intended to veil his impotence. Kumalo then goes to the village schoolmaster, who is equally helpless. Kumalo is "dispirited and depressed," wondering how he may serve his village as a priest and if the problems his parishioners face are "beyond all helping." But he is not in despair. "No power but the power of God could bring about such a miracle, and he prayed again briefly, Into Thy hands, oh God, I commend Indotsheni." (233) As always in *Cry, the Beloved Country*, faith is facilitative and prayer is answered. The miracle Kumalo hopes for is delivered, and in such a way as to show that good men's works are the necessary vehicles for the miracles God is called upon to perform. This is precisely what Kumalo had realized when he had first prayed "for the restoration of Ndotsheni."

After commending everything to God's hands, Kumalo leaves his church, goes into his house, and begins to work on the church account books. But he hears the sound of a horse's hooves, and

> [h]e rose from his chair, and went out to see who might be riding in the merciless sun. And for a moment he caught his breath in astonishment, for it was a small white boy on a red horse, a small white boy as like to another who had ridden here as any could be. (233)

First appearing to be a vision, what Kumalo sees is quite concrete. The miraculous event is enclosed within the form of a perfectly ordinary event. The spirit of Arthur returns in the form of his son, and Kumalo goes to meet it. The boy greets Kumalo respectfully, as if he were unaware of the social distinction that favors him, and Kumalo greets him. They begin to speak, and the boy asks to see the inside of Kumalo's home. Kumalo takes him inside and offers him a drink of water. The boy says, however: "I would like a drink of milk.... Ice cold, from the fridge." The conversation continues:

> —Inkosana [little master], there is no fridge in Ndotsheni.
> —Just ordinary milk then, umfundisi.
> —Inkosana, there is no milk in Ndotsheni.
> The small boy flushed. I would like water, umfundisi, he said.
> Kumalo brought him the water. (235)

The two then continue to speak, and the boy tells Kumalo the Zulu word for water, and several other words he knows in Zulu, and Kumalo praises and encourages him. When the boy realizes it is time to go, he thanks Kumalo for the water and says he will return to talk more Zulu. But before he goes—having experienced the virtue of feeling shame when he blushed at the realization of his privilege—the boy asks: "Why is there no milk in Ndotsheni? Is it because the people are very poor?" Kumalo answers that it is so, and the conversation continues:

> —And what do the children do?
> Kumalo looked at him. They die, my child, he said. Some of them are dying now.
> —Who is dying?
> —The small one of Kulse.
> —Didn't the doctor come?
> —Yes, he came.
> —And what did he say?
> —He said the child must have milk, inkosana.
> —And what did the parents say?
> —They said, Doctor, we have heard what you say.
> And the small boy said in a small voice, I see. (236–237)

On the heels of the boy's appearance comes the first phase of the miracle, as Kumalo's prayers for Ndotsheni are answered. That evening, while Kumalo and his family "were having their meal ... there was a sound of wheels, and a knock on the door." It is one of the villagers. Kumalo invites him to eat with them. He responds:

> —No indeed. I am on my way home. I have a message for you ... from Jarvis. Was the small white boy here today?
> Kumalo had a dull sense of fear, realizing for the first time what he had done.
> —He was here, he said.
> —We were working in the trees, said the man, when this small boy came riding up. I do not understand English, umfundisi, but they were talking about Kuluse's child. And come and look what I have brought you.
> There outside was the milk. (237)

It is the first of many deeds of grace that Jarvis performs in the final chapters (**32–36**) led by Arthur's spirit and Arthur's child and his own enlightened heart. He begins an entire land reclamation project, bringing in surveyors to build a dam to irrigate the land so that it will grow green and abundant, that there may be milk and farming. He also brings in an agricultural demonstrator to teach the villagers how to farm and how to avoid erosion, and he pays for the building of a new church in Ndotsheni. Arthur's son continues to visit Kumalo, ostensibly to learn to speak Zulu, but more because a bond of affection has grown up between the two. And a model of social progress is created founded on a spiritual harmony that obliterates racial differences and recognizes the brotherhood of all, the consequent interdependence of all, and the mutual responsibility of all for all. Jarvis quite literally begins to follow the biblical injunction to sell all he has and give to the poor. As they are working on the dam, Kumalo hears the white magistrate say of Jarvis: "They say he's going quite queer. From what I've heard, he soon won't have any money left." (243)

Hope Beyond Sight

Cry, the Beloved Country is a novel that grows out of and reflects the system of South African racial injustice. But it is, perhaps, even more, a novel that uses that blighted system as a means of revealing the transcendent message of faith—which is hope that goes beyond the capacity of present sight—and brotherhood, and the presence of God in the good actions of individuals. When Kumalo calls the agricultural teacher an angel from God or Arthur's son a little angel from God, or the letter Jarvis sends him after his wife dies, assuring him that he will rebuild the church and that his wife had been ill even before Arthur's murder, (that Kumalo's soul need not be burdened with her death) a letter from God, he is not speaking in metaphor. He means it literally, and he expresses not the unreliable perception of a character within a novel, but the essential vision of the novel itself, that the grace of God and the abundance of Nature are accomplished through the works of mankind. The engine that powers this work, Paton proposes in *Cry, the Beloved Country*, is love, and the force that inhibits it is fear. And the only way to overcome fear, the only way it can be "cast out," is "by love." Thus Paton ends his moral tale not only with a condemnation of injustice and the simple truth "that men should walk upright in the land where they were born, and be free to use the fruits of the earth," (276) but with an exhortation to love one another because without that love this practical truth, given the tangles of fear, hatred and greed, is a paradisiacal wish. Social as the focus of the story has been, in the end the burden is on each individual to continue in love and hope despite the evils which tempt one to despair. Jarvis, bereft, but inspired by the transcendental vision of his son's teaching and by the intensity of suffering he has seen in Kumalo's face—which made him recognize Kumalo's humanity, their common brotherhood, and therefore his own human duties—takes up the work of restoring the land, and on the eve of Absalom's execution he shares Kumalo's grief for the loss of the boy who killed his own son. And Kumalo, a hero of suffering, endurance, and faith, on a hilltop in Ndotsheni, far from his son on the morning of his execution, prays and watches for the dawn, which marks his son's death and the birth of a new day. He is sustained by faith and the work he has undertaken to continue in the benighted present, work which gives substance to that faith and reality to his hope.

> And while he stood there the sun rose in the east.... For it is the dawn that has come, as it has come for a thousand centuries, never failing. But when that dawn will come, of our emancipation, from the fear of bondage and the bondage of fear, why, that is secret. (277)

Critical Views

HORTON DAVIES ON INSPIRATION

The decisive element in [the] religious interpretation [of *Cry, the Beloved Country*] is, of course, the central Christian doctrine of the Incarnation, the stooping of God in Christ to conquer our humanity, to gather to himself all the prodigals of our race by the sheerly sacrificial and forgiving love of the Cross. Christ the Lord as Everyman's Friend is the inspiration of Paton's own faith, and the impetus to a transformed racial and social order. Faith is to replace fear, and service domination. "Perfect love casteth out fear" and "the love of Christ constrains us." Paton shows in his novel the creative possibilities of forgiveness as he records the moving visit of the African priest, Stephen Kumalo, to the house of Mr Jarvis, senior: the former's son has murdered the latter's, but even the pain of this excruciating situation is relieved by an acceptance of the Divine forgiveness evoking human forgiveness. Paton could say with Reinhold Niebuhr, "Forgiveness is the crown of Christian ethics." Paton's living faith in the crucified and risen Lord gives him balance: it makes him chary of purely humanistic utopias, while it delivers him from the despair of social reformers trusting in the fundamental goodness of human nature alone. He is both this-worldly (to stave off individualistic pietism) and other-worldly (to keep pragmatism at bay). The Church is for him the home of the friends of Christ, a supernatural family united in the worship of God in a shrine where temporal distinctions of race or class or sex are transcended. The realism of his understanding of the demonic dimensions of unregenerate human nature, and his unquenchable hope of reform, spring directly from his understanding of the Christian revelation. The theologically-inspired sociology is the message of his book.
[...]

It is time to turn to the artistry of the novel. What were the sources of his inspiration and craftsmanship? Clearly, they were his experience of life in a multi-racial community such as South Africa is, but experience coloured by his Christian ideals and his own reading and thinking. Familiar with the classics of English literature (especially Thomas Hardy), he is particularly fond of the great Russian novelists, Dostoievsky and Tolstoi. Of contemporary novelists, he finds Thomas Wolfe, Charles Morgan, Robert Gibbings and Graham Greene most congenial and stimulating. In poetry his comprehensive reading embraces both the virility and enthusiasm of Walt Whitman and the religious insights, sensibility, technical mastery and massive culture of T. S. Eliot.

It is almost always dangerous to attempt to find the originals of characters in a novel, particularly so when traits derived from several persons are amalgamated to form one character-sketch, written larger than life. For the novelist is a selective artist, not a photographer. No doubt the model for Shakespeare's Falstaff would have failed to recognise himself as the amiable, fat, foolish knight of *The Merry Wives*, for in his own imaginatively-intoxicated mind he was a compound of Romeo and Henry V at Agincourt. Despite the warning, there are some clear clues to the originals of some of the characters in *Cry, the Beloved Country*, and such literary detection is always interesting. (Perhaps the author will forgive the essayist this lapse from grace as Mr Paton is an avid reader of Mr Freeman Wills Crofts's detective fiction!) Father Trevor Huddlestone, the moving spirit in the Rosettenville House of the Community of the Resurrection, a consistent champion of the rights of Africans for Christ's sake, was the model for the sympathetic portrait of Father Vincent. The physical outline of Kumalo was provided by an old man who used to visit Diepkloof Reformatory. The young man in the novel who exhibited such concern for and understanding of his charges is modelled on the Probation Officer at Diepkloof who is in charge of the replacement of released pupils. Perhaps the most interesting identification of all is that of Arthur Jarvis, the studious social reformer, with the author himself. The wide interests of the man and the very titles of his cherished library and the significant portraits on the wall of his study, these are as autobiographical as the social credo (pp. 150–1) and ethical platform of Alan Paton (pp. 168–9).

The style, the characterisation and the theme of *Cry, the Beloved Country* are all outstanding. The simple, inverted, almost Biblical diction of the Zulus recalls the rendering of Welsh idioms by inversion in Richard Llewellyn's admirable *How Green was my Valley*. How superbly both these novelists evoke nostalgia for a simpler, more wholesome way of life before industrialisation had broken up family life! Alan Paton makes a poem out of soil erosion:

> The great red hills stand desolate and the earth has torn away like flesh. The lightning flashes over them, the clouds pour down upon them, the dead streams come to life, full of the red blood of the earth.

The torn earth is a mirror of torn humanity, uprooted from its tribal contacts with good mother earth. This flexible and varied style is now taut, concise, telegrammatic when describing the social dustbin that is Shanty Town; now soaring into pure poetry when evocative of the delights of the South African countryside; now suitably turbid, when weighted with emotional content, and impassioned. Indeed, sometimes we are reading a documentary and sometimes a romance, and the two themes and styles are deftly interwoven in Chapter Nine of Book One, when the repeated question of the woman searching for a home and the equally insistent negatives to her plea sound like a Greek chorus. There is often a subtle use of symbols, too. One recalls, for instance, the scene of Kumalo playing with his little nephew, seeing in him the image of his lost son and that son's lost innocence. Similarly there are two levels of meaning, when soil erosion symbolises soul erosion.

The theme is as remarkable as the mood, which is not one of accusation but of pathos, "calm of mind, all passion spent." "To know all is to forgive all," and to repent, seems to be the artist's theme. Kumalo is not a tragic hero, in the classical mould, for he has no fatal flaw, no *hamartia*, which brings his own downfall. But his significance is not individual, but representative. He is a stricken member of a dying society brought low by detribalisation and the grasping materialism of the dominant white group. Kumalo is therefore more significant as part of a social tragedy than any individual downfall could be. Lear is a great tragic figure of Titanic mould, but Shakespeare cannot teach us sociological lessons from his fall. Paton's aim is different; possibly more relevant to twentieth-century needs. Though he, too, hopes for a cathartic effect upon his readers.

Each reader will have his own anthology of favourite scenes or passages, but all, I judge, will be agreed on the variety and vividness of the work as a whole. For sheer poetry the first chapters of both Book One and Book Two are unapproachable. In the first passage, already cited, the rotting land mirrors a dying African society. (Again the parallel with *King Lear* holds, where Nature in her most ruthless mood magnifies the pathos of Lear, emotionally storm-tossed and as insignificant as a sere leaf driven by Heaven's rage.) With this romantic quality, should be contrasted his "documentary" technique as seen, for instance, in Book Two, Chapter Nine. Here he records John Kumalo's harangue to the underprivileged Africans, the spate and hate of the demagogue, and the different responses it evokes from the bystanders: the admiration of the inarticulate Africans whose spokesman he is, the snarling impatience of the white listeners, and the sympathetic but anxious reaction of the author himself. This multiple response holds the mirror up to the racial tensions of South Africa.

Then, again, the superb interview of Father Vincent, the white priest, with the African priest, Father Stephen Kumalo, is a highlight of the story. Here religious deep calls to deep and the technique of a patient, loving, but firm confessor is admirably expounded. The wise English priest lets his brother minister in perplexity pour out his spate of words until their momentum comes to an end. He interjects only the brief consoling words, "my friend." He suggests kindly, but firmly, that Kumalo's concern must be not with his own sorrow, but with his son's amendment. He then recommends positive action: Kumalo is to pray for all who need prayer, to lose his personal sorrow in the wide need of the world and to give thanks. Finally, he promises to pray for Kumalo himself and to help him in every possible way. This part of the drama is spiritually perfect. The contrast between the agonised mind of the African priest and the assurance and patience of the faith of the English priest could not be bettered. Paton succeeds in that most difficult of tasks—making goodness seem not only attractive, but inevitable.

For sheer delicacy in the handling of pathos and in the exposition of a creative mutual forgiveness, it would be difficult to find a better example than the encounter, already mentioned, of Stephen Kumalo and the father of Arthur Jarvis. Here indeed are thoughts that lie too deep for tears.

The climax of the story, though not its end, is the Trial and Judgment scenes. Here the contrast between the inflexibility and the majesty of the Law, and the plight of the accused African is finely sustained. The irony of the complicity of the European society in the crime of the African is subtly suggested, too.

Perhaps the greatest tribute to Paton's artistry, apart from the fact that it deserves and repays re-reading, is that the author has, by the sheer skill of his delineation and his deep interest in his representative characters, overcome some formidable technical obstacles. Soliloquies, speeches, meditations, long descriptive passages, social reports and manifestoes of faith, can all too easily become burdensome. That they did not, is due to the burning sincerity of the writer and the urgent electricity with which he charges these passages of prose.

Paton's message is found in the concluding, interrupted postscript of Arthur Jarvis:

Is it strange that our civilisation is riddled through and through with dilemmas? The truth is that our civilisation is not Christian; it is a tragic compound of great ideal and fearful practice, of high assurance and desperate anxiety, of loving charity and fearful clutching of possessions. Allow me a minute ...

Paton's reformer was not allowed his minute, for death interrupted his *credo*. We trust that Alan Paton will be allowed not minutes nor hours, but long years in which to disturb us—in novel, poetry and biography—into a more resolute attempt to resolve the tensions between our Christian ideals and our contemporary practice.

SHERIDAN BAKER ON THE BOOK AS MORAL GEOGRAPHY

Alan Paton's *Cry, the Beloved Country* (1948) has earned a place in our literature, at least in the classroom, but as yet has invited no explication. I should like to approach the book as a kind of moral geography, since Paton's title itself shows the land articulate. Kumalo's trials and African sociology all take their ultimate meanings in geographical symbols; and Paton has, in fact, even readjusted South Africa's profile to resemble that moral terrain which both Bunyan and Dante traveled and of which every man knows something, I think, though he has read neither.

Paton does this by allusions both Biblical and primitive. His language leads to the hills, cities, valleys, and green pastures we connect with right and wrong, even when scriptural references are not direct. But Paton uses a moral sensing of geography even more primitive: the sense perhaps in all creatures grounded by gravity that up and down are, by nature, good and bad, that mountains are upright and valleys submissive, that we stand up to live and lie down to die.

Of course, we lie down to rest, too. The valley is a somewhat ambiguous cradle, a nourisher of what Paton calls "deep feelings." Valleys represent maternal comfort and comfortable death; hills, paternal threat and protection. The mountain shadows the valley, brings thunder and water, and has inaccessible heights where the Unknowns live. And a man on the way up is better off than one on the way down. These primeval ups and downs, I think, still alive in our idiom with ambiguities intact, underlie Paton's symbolism.

Paton's moral geography is this: (1) a good valley which has cradled us but which, from social decay and drought, is also the valley of the shadow of death, (2) a beautiful mountain looking down on the valley, sending water and hope, the peak of Omniscience, (3) the city of the plain. The valley is Ndotsheni, the tribal home of the black Reverend Stephen Kumalo. The mountain we may call Carisbrooke, the point at which the reader enters the book to look down on Kumalo's world, the home of the white James Jarvis. The city of the plain is Johannesburg, where black and white pour trouble together:

> Water comes out of a bottle, till the glass is full. Then the lights go out. And when they come on again, to the bottle is full and upright, and the glass empty.... Black and white, it says, black and white, though it is red and green. (p. 17, Modern Standard Authors ed.)

Johannesburg's evil has broken the tribe. There Kumalo's sister sells her whiskey and herself. The green valley of home now runs only red earth when it rains, for energy has shifted to Johannesburg. There black and white collide in violence, which at last miraculously causes water to flow from Carisbrooke down to Ndotsheni.

Because we see mostly through Kumalo's primitive eyes, the symbolism of mountain and valley comes naturally to Paton's book. Kumalo is "a Zulu schooled in English" (15), a Zulu wearing an Anglican collar. The language we are to suppose is Zulu takes on the rhythms and phrases of the English Bible, which Kumalo, of course, uses in its Zulu version. An English priest tells a parable "in that symbolic language that is like the Zulu tongue" (108), and we realize that both languages are simple, concrete and figurative, the language of tribes living close to the land. The book's idiom both represents and resolves, as does Kumalo himself, the black–white dilemma:

> ... Now God be thanked that there is a beloved one who can lift up the heart in suffering, that one can play with a child in the face of such misery. Now God be thanked

that the name of a hill is such music, that the name of a river can heal. Aye, even the name of a river that runs no more.

... But this, the purpose of our lives, the end of all our struggle, is beyond all human wisdom. Oh God, my God, do not Thou forsake me. Yea, though I walk through the valley of the shadow of death, I shall fear no evil, if Thou art with me.... (62)

The valley of the shadow of death, indeed, is both the valley of Ndotsheni and Kumalo's personal loss of a son, the hope of the primitive tribe where "the dead streams come to life, full of the red blood of the earth" (4). As Kumalo says, only God can save it (233).

But God saves Ndotsheni in the person of James Jarvis, who lives on the beautiful mountain and likewise loses a son to the world. We are told that the ground Jarvis farms is holy; its name is High Place. And whether or not Paton intends "Jarvis" to remind us of "Jahveh" or "Jehovah," we soon find him sitting on a stone at the mountaintop, like an Old Testament God, overlooking the world, remote yet troubled by it. Throughout the book Jarvis receives incidental references as God—a letter from him is a "letter from God" (262), his grandson is "a small angel from God" (249), his son is admired "as though he were God Almighty" (139), and so forth. Moreover, his son has gone into the world of Johannesburg; he takes up a mission of mercy; he is killed by the very people he comes to save. And through the father the dead son works a Christian miracle: suffered love makes evil good. Jarvis, even like God, does not really become effective until he learns compassion from the loss of his son.

Through these readings, then, Paton works his magic on the mountain at Carisbrooke. The more clearly we see Jarvis as God, the more we see Carisbrooke's supernatural height. The more Jarvis grows in understanding and goodness, the more we see the mountain as symbol of these qualities. But the figurative Godhead which accumulates behind Jarvis does not overshadow Jarvis the man, and, conversely, ordinary events, under Paton's scriptural spell, take on heavenly illumination without losing substance. Kumalo's Biblical vision—emanating from the beautiful mountain—illustrates Paton's ability to give the modern world an easy traffic with the age of miracles. An automobile, not a chariot, swings low, and the effect is in no way ludicrous:

> While he stood there he saw a motor car coming down the road from Carisbrooke into the valley. It was a sight seldom seen.... Then he saw that not far from the church there was a white man sitting still upon a horse. He seemed to be waiting for the car, and with something of a shock he realized that it was Jarvis. (241)

One suspects that black men converted to Christianity by white men picture God as white, Marc Connelly notwithstanding, and that Paton's symbolic use of Jarvis is particularly apt.

Jarvis's personal growth is paralleled by Kumalo's until at the end of the book Kumalo replaces Jarvis on the mountain. Kumalo, too, has a son. In fact, all sons, in Paton's book, bring salvation. The dying valley which runs blood and is resurrected represents the death of both sons, all death, and the life which springs therefrom. The grandson, the nephew, the unborn son, children on their way to school (as if trailing clouds of glory) "coming down from the hills, dropping sometimes out of the very mist" (61)—all bring comfort and hope.

But Kumalo's son brings salvation only at one remove. He kills Jarvis's son, evil making good apparent, black vivifying white. The white son represents the unshakable power of good, transcending death, even increasing; the black son—a kind of Antichrist—represents the hapless innocence of evil in a drifting society. The collision of the two first brings the fathers pain, then mutual sympathy, then some understanding of the good that works in spite of everything. Kumalo's salvation is harder than Jarvis's, and Paton puts his readers closer to Kumalo the Man than to Jarvis the God. Jarvis immediately begins to read his way into the mystery of a good son murdered. But Kumalo has no such comfort. His son is a frightened child, with only a strand of truthfulness left, guilty of mortal sin. Absalom's crime shows Kumalo the hard fact that society may seem the cause but that the individual is responsible. And Kumalo must absorb this bitterness before he can accept the good which flows through the world, even from this tangle. Losing his beloved yet sinning Absalom—a figurative rebel against the righteous father—Kumalo is changed from a kind of primitive tribal leader into the New Testament Father his priesthood indicates. The loss of both sons, the antithesis of both, causes water and milk to flow from High Place down to Ndotsheni, the valley of the shadow, which is, also, this world.

Paton's ancient paradigm of hill and valley as heaven and earth grows clearer as the book progresses. But the more symbolic High Place and Ndotsheni become, the stronger becomes Paton's suggestion that they are Ideals only, remote yet seen, contours to steer by. Only in the evil world is the Son's sacrifice possible and effective. The simple ups and downs of the country are not enough:

> Cry, the beloved country, for the unborn child that is the inheritor of our fear. Let him not love the earth too deeply ... nor give too much of his heart to a mountain or a valley. For fear will rob him of all if he gives too much. (80)

Arthur Jarvis first learned to love Africa when, as a boy, he rode "over green hills and into the great valleys" (174), but the city on the plain taught him their meaning. It is in evil Johannesburg that Kumalo says, "I have never met such kindness" (125)—"I have known no one as you are" (215). And Kumalo brings his heightened and deepened perception back to the symbolic mountain and valley.

We come to see that the country represents man and the city represents men. The most insistent image in Paton's book is that of a man—first Jarvis, then Kumalo—alone on a mountain brooding over the depths. Carisbrooke and Ndotsheni denominate the human spirit. Johannesburg is a flat turbulence of good and evil which makes distinctions difficult. Johannesburg is a sociological casebook, with stopgap plans and masses of men. The country is man consulting his soul and learning human inadequacy. When Kumalo comes back from Johannesburg with a son lost and notions of rebuilding the tribe, he consults the ineffective chief and the ineffective schoolmaster. He is left with no one but himself, and prayer and God, finally to rebuild the valley and climb the mountain.

The mountain frames the book at either end. From the first sentence we can feel Paton's moral pressure, and we soon notice that it has indeed remolded the South African landscape. A map will show that Paton's beloved country has gently heightened and deepened until it quite contradicts the earth's hard surface. We are surprised to find that Johannesburg, at 5,764 feet, is actually more than a thousand feet higher than our high mountain in Natal, which, though heightened each time Paton returns to it, seemed even at first almost the top of the world. In his opening passage, other mountains seem not higher but merely "beyond and behind"; the great Drakensberg range with peaks over 10,000 feet, behind which lies Johannesburg on its high plateau, is merely a place beyond, with no height at all. We are on a mountain that touches the clouds.

The contradiction between morally-high Carisbrooke and actually-higher Johannesburg works Paton no embarrassment. He can even take brief moral advantage of Johannesburg's altitude, suggesting a civilization and complexity looming over simple life along the Umzimkulu. Kumalo's brother speaks both literally and scornfully of his old home as "down." Indeed, Paton makes the city of the plain momentarily higher than it really is. Approaching Johannesburg, he emphasizes climbing: "Climb up to Hilton ... ," he writes, "Climb over the Drakensberg, on to the level plains" (15). The level plains seem like the top of a table, reached after much climbing, and so this new country seems to back-country Kumalo, overwhelmed by buildings and buses. But Paton has matched his plain to Kumalo's awe, for, actually, after crossing the Drakensberg at more than eight thousand feet, we drop back down some three thousand feet to Johannesburg, though we do not drop so far as the mountain top from which we started.

Nevertheless, with the mountain at Carisbrooke as reference first for the Beautiful then for the Good, we come to think of Johannesburg as sprawling somewhere on a plain even lower than the home valley. And Paton helps us to this illusion. Leaving Carisbrooke, the train suspends us in unreality. We start in the mist. "The train passes through a world of fancy" (11). Finally, sleep separates primitive heights from the city on the plain.

Furthermore, Johannesburg's relative flatness depresses its actual altitude. On the plain Kumalo sees "great white dumps of the mines, like hills under the sun" (181). He hears of buildings as high as "the hill that stands so, straight up, behind my father's kraal" (16). He sees wheels high in the air. And when we are in Johannesburg, in spite of one street corner on a hill (47), in spite of walking "up Twist Street" and "down Louis Botha" (44), the mind keeps the city flat. With Kumalo's thoughts we return to hills, and the hills now seem higher, no matter how the land really lies. His return trip repeats unreality and separation (note especially the stagecraft in "rolls away"): "The white flat hills of the mines drop behind, and the country rolls away as far as the eye can see (219)." Again sleep leaves one world behind.

Paton can now afford to wind explicitly down the Drakensberg because from Pietermaritzburg he can carry his readers up and up again, into the heights at Carisbrooke. This trip from Pietermaritzburg to Carisbrooke helps to explain the slightly puzzling road that begins the book: "There is a lovely road that runs from Ixopo into the hills...." Why do we start from Ixopo, never more than a passing reference, why on the road to Carisbrooke rather than at Carisbrooke itself, Paton's essential scene? There is no reason intrinsic to the book, only the reason in Paton himself. He was born in "Pietermaritzburg, the lovely city." Carisbrooke is the point of vision, we infer, toward which Paton climbed as boy and man. It is not his home. It is in the hills beyond, higher, wilder, removed from daily streets, a point to dream from. "All roads lead to

Johannesburg," he writes (10, 52)—even the one going into the hills in the opposite direction, for so we assume it was in the growth of this man who began life in Pietermaritzburg, taught school in Ixopo, hiked on up to Carisbrooke, turned around to revolutionize a reformatory in Johannesburg, and poured his experience into his book a generation later. Pietermaritzburg is really the place from which, as we enter the book, we are taking our run into spiritual hills, and Kumalo comes home to the good hills of Paton's own experience.

The book ends as it began, at Carisbrooke, though on the peak just above it. From here we first looked down at Ndotsheni and its comic-pathetic little priest, with his dirty collar and leaky church—grand in the eyes of a child—the rustic who fears traffic lights and admires a bus driver's courage. But Kumalo has grown. He himself has even learned amusement at his friend and at Jarvis and the mystery of goodness (238). When he climbs to the mountain he is no longer beneath us; the truth of his experience comes to us directly, at the white reader's own superior altitude. Here, at this new height, Kumalo replaces Jarvis as God the Father, and the hill at Carisbrooke, actually lower than Johannesburg, has now towered up to heaven itself.

Kumalo goes up the mountain to wait for the dawn that will see his son hanged in Praetoria. We think of Christ going into the wilderness, and of Moses, who talked to God on mountains: "But even as he started to climb the path that ran through the great stones, a man on a horse was there, and a voice said to him, it is you, umfundisi?—It is I umnumzana" (271).

Jarvis goes down the mountain, Kumalo climbs to the top, sits on a stone, and takes Jarvis's position, "looking out over the great valley." Here, above the place where Jarvis first suffered the news or his son's death, Kumalo waits for the sunrise signaling *his* son's execution for the sins of the world.

For, though Absalom is a murderer and we see him childish and frightened, Paton traces suggestions of Christ behind him nevertheless. Father Vincent, referring to Absalom, says, "There was a thief upon the cross" (109). We remember that

Christ, too, was executed as a criminal. Absalom is betrayed; there are three culprits; like Christ naming his successor, Absalom wishes his son named Peter. On the Mount of Olives, Christ, like Absalom, prayed his Father not to let him die: "Father, if thou be willing, remove this cup from me: Nevertheless not my will, but thine, be done" (Luke 22:42). Absalom in prison falls before his father "crouched in the way that some of the Indians pray" (207). Kumalo, on the mountain, remembers his words, the conventional Zulu responses: "it is as my father wishes, it is as my father says" (273).

The structure is complete: the two fathers, the two sons, the two mountains, as it were, at beginning and end. It is the black Father, with the compassion of the white man's suffering God, to whom Paton leaves the hope of Africa, and its misgivings, on the highest spiritual mountain imaginable—God in a heaven painful because compassionate, witnessing his son's death and resurrection: "And when he expected it, he rose to his feet and took off his hat and laid it down on the earth, and clasped his hands before him. And while he stood there the sun rose in the east" (277).

The morality Paton writes into his geography, then, is Christian: the salvage of evil through love and suffering. But the geographical pulls are primitive, compelling South Africa's actual geography to match their moral ups and downs. The moral heights of Carisbrooke are Paton's dominant symbol. There we begin and there we end, heightened by a kind of kinesthetic moral experience among mountains and valleys long built into our imagining by literature and gravity.

EDMUND FULLER ON TRAGEDY

Cry, the Beloved Country is tragic, but is not a tragedy in the formal literary sense, and it carries the clear affirmation of an element transcending the tragic view of life. This element is Christian, but it is not only in Christianity that such transcendence of tragedy is possible. That most tightly implacable of the Greek tragedies, *Oedipus Tyrannus*, is followed by the mystical transcendence of *Oedipus at Colonnus*. Again in a Christian frame, there are transcendent elements at the close of *The Brothers Karamazov* which would have come to flower in the projected further novel about Alyosha which Dostoyevsky did not live to write.

In *Cry, the Beloved Country* the primary story is pathetic, in that the suffering characters are more bewildered victims than prime movers in their difficulties. The tragic elements are social, and as always, complexly interlocked in cause and effect. The destruction of the soil, the breaking of the tribal system and the home, the tight segregation of South African society producing ghetto slums, the compound system in the mines, the provocative juxtaposition of the haves and the have-nots: these are the specific and local social factors working upon the general and universal human nature. The story is fiction, but Paton says in an Author's Note, "as a social record it is the plain and simple truth."

The shock effects of a cultural frontier are not unique to Africa. Interesting parallel elements can be seen in Oliver LaFarge's *Laughing Boy*, in terms of the American Indians. When any tribal system is shattered by the white man, but the tribal people are not taken into the white man's culture, deterioration and tragedy are inevitable. The African priest Msimangu, in Johannesburg, one of the compelling figures of the book, says,

> The tragedy is not that things are broken. The tragedy is that they are not mended again. The white man has broken the tribe. And it is my belief ... that it cannot be mended again.

Cry, the Beloved Country is a splendid piece of craftsmanship, extraordinary as a first book by a man in middle life, whose work had been in education and penology. The most jaded reviewers were won by the fresh, individual lyricism of its style and the passion of its conviction and its thirst for justice. Paton's use of idioms and rhythms from Zulu, Bantu, Xosa and

Afrikaans speech contributed greatly to the fresh effect. Now that his work is well known, and now that other writers have used these language patterns, Paton's style still has its personal stamp, and we must not let familiarity dull our recollection of its first invigorating impact.

The book is skillfully constructed in parallels. The simple African Anglican priest, Stephen Kumalo, loses his son, Absalom. The African-English farmer, James Jarvis, loses his son, Arthur. It is Absalom who kills Arthur, for which the state kills Absalom.

By the keenest of the ironies in which the book is rich, Arthur Jarvis was among the greatest friends of the black man, in the forefront of the struggle for justice. The senseless tragedy that links the two sons ultimately links the two fathers. There is no finer scene in a consistently moving book than that in which Stephen Kumalo and James Jarvis first come face to face, by chance, after the shooting, and realize one another's identities.

The ramifications of the story are comprehensive, showing the life of the tribal country and of the city. Through Stephen's journey to Johannesburg to search for his sister and his son, we see how that city, with its mine compounds and shantytown slums, swallows up people and breeds criminals. The quest involves a vivid tour of the native districts, and of the reformatory of which Paton himself had been superintendent. In interpolated meditations on the courts, and upon a new gold field, he deepens the social texture. Most adroit touch of all: the papers and speeches and books of the dead Arthur Jarvis are made the medium of direct polemical statement, and also of growth in the character of James Jarvis.

The father had not approved or understood his son's position on the race question. One could have imagined an implacable hardening on the issue after the tragedy, as would have been found in a temperament like Jacob van Vlanderen's: "I always told him he was a fool—and now one of the so-and-so's has shot him!" Instead, the grace that gradually works in James Jarvis is that of love, for he had loved the young man, even without comprehending him. When he is exposed to his son's papers, in the solitude of grief, he finds him for the first time and perceives that to repudiate his son's principles now will be truly to lose him utterly. By honoring and carrying forward his son's actions, something is retained that cannot be lost even in death. It is a measure both of the man, and of the remedial power of love. The new James Jarvis is "a man who put his feet upon a road, and ... no man would turn him from it."

Among the central threads of the book is the question of Stephen Kumalo's response to his son's guilt, as contrasted to the attitude of his politician-brother, John Kumalo, toward his own son's involvement as an accessory in the shooting.

John Kumalo, whose experience of the city has led him to cast off the faith, is solely concerned with evading punishment for his son and trouble for himself. He is aware that the boy was present, but is successful in obtaining his acquittal through perjury. In John's terms, he has been successful, but we expect that the last state will be worse than the first. The prospects are not bright for his son.

Stephen, on the other hand, faces a profound discovery. Once his son's guilt is established, it is impossible for him, as a Christian, to seek to evade punishment. His most urgent concern is for his son's repentance. He sees that Absalom, whose, name, "his father's peace," is as ironic for Kumalo as it had been for King David, is more unhappy that he has been caught than for what he has done. To lead the boy to repentance becomes his first aim. For the Christian, ultimate welfare is not a question of the life or death of the body, but the life or death of the soul.

Repentance is validated by the acceptance of punishment. After the confessed guilt, after the accepted punishment, then mercy (in men's terms) may or may not be forthcoming. But mercy is not to be given on sentimental impulse. Mercy follows judgment; it does not precede it.

John Kumalo would save his son's life and does not believe in his soul. Stephen would be grateful for his son's life, but would not wish it bartered for his soul. At the end, there is hope for Absalom's repentance—though only God can judge of it.

Gertrude, Stephen's sister, whose degraded state had been the direct cause of Stephen's summons to Johannesburg, is lost. She has gone beyond her personal point of return. The effort of self-examination and rehabilitation is more than she can sustain. She slips away, just before the return of the little party of family survivors to the home village of Ndotsheni.

Yet there is salvage from the loss and pain. It is this that leads Paton beyond tragedy and that prompts the subtitle of the book: "A Story of Comfort in Desolation." If Absalom has repented, he has not lost both life and soul, as he had been in the way to do. Carried back to Ndotsheni (the account of their arrival is a magnificent lyrical passage), from the certainty of loss in Johannesburg to the possibility of new life, are Gertrude's son, Absalom's wife, and her unborn child. Stephen Kumalo and James Jarvis are enlarged in spirit, and from the spirit come works that promise the renewal of the land around Ndotsheni.

MARTIN TUCKER ON THE NOVEL OF FORGIVENESS

The most famous and one of the earliest novels of forgiveness is Alan Paton's *Cry, the Beloved Country*. This work and [Olive Schteiner's] *The Story of an African Farm* are the two best-known novels' in English—with a South African locale—to readers outside South Africa. Ironically, though Paton's novel has spawned a host of imitations and has been highly praised as propaganda, most contemporary South African writers deny any literary indebtedness to Paton. Yet *Cry, the Beloved Country* is at least as well-written a novel as the many novels which have followed its lead. Today also, Paton's humanism is being attacked as old-fashioned and sentimental. Ezekiel Mphahlele has accused Paton of falsifying human nature because in his view Paton divides people into good and bad and then lays on these cardboard figures a heavy liberalism and a "monumental sermon."[31] Peter Abrahams, in reviewing *South African Predicament: The Economics of Apartheid* (London, 1960) by F. P. Spooner, commented:

In the main, social, political and economic studies on South Africa (as well as practically all the fiction) have been written by people who are not in step with the prevailing mood of the majority of white South Africans: people like Alan Paton represent a tiny fractional minority viewpoint in the broad spectrum of general white South African opinion on the problems facing that unhappy country.... The denunciation, unlike that of the Alan Paton minority, is not that apartheid is evil and immoral and socially wrong. They (and Mr. Spooner is one of their most intelligent spokesmen) denounce apartheid because it will not work.[32]

In *Cry, the Beloved Country* the ways of justice and God are mysterious, but in the person of Paton's central character love brings an acceptance that explains nothing while meaning all. Stephen Kumalo, a Christian Zulu minister from the hill country of Ixopo, travels to Johannesburg to rescue his sister and his son: his sister has become a whore, and his son a murderer, while Kumalo's brother has forsaken Christianity for atheism and the political force of trade unionism. Kumalo's journey is abortive, yet it is not entirely fruitless. Though the son is executed by the State, the father of the murderer and the father of the murdered son join hands in friendship. Ironically, the murdered man was a white liberal who was writing a report, "The Truth About Native Crime," at the time of his death.

The novel is at least one report on this truth about native crime. The murderer was a boy unable to resist the temptation of the big city. In the hill country he was a decent boy; in the big city he is easy prey for criminals, who exploit his ignorance and gullibility for their own ends. The first half of the novel ends with the return home of Kumalo to the hill country, where his Christian message of love still dominates.

The second half of the novel has had a profound influence on the thoughts of non-South African readers, even if its message is currently being derided by some black South African literary critics. For Paton's novel is the supreme example of the kind of novel of forgiveness which calls for the construction of love on the ruins of tragedy. The father of the murdered man comes to the humble church where Kumalo preaches in order to say good-bye before leaving for Johannesburg. Kumalo thanks him for the large donation he has given for the reconstruction of the church roof. The white man says, "I have seen a man who was in darkness till you found him. If that is what you do, I give it willingly." And as the white man leaves, each cries to the other, "Go well, go well" (p. 268). This lyric to the suffering of Africa, the portrait of the long hard road to understanding is simply, gracefully expressed in biblical rhythms.

Notes

31. See *The African Image* (London, 1982), pp. 131–33.
32. *New York Times Book Review* (October 22, 1981), p. 3.

MYRON MATLAW ON STYLISTIC UNDERSTATEMENT

The emotional impact of *Cry, the Beloved Country* is achieved, first of all and most consistently, by Paton's stylistic understatement, by his use and reuse of a few simple, almost stilted, formal phrases. *Is it heavy?* Jarvis asks Stephen Kumalo when the latter haltingly and painfully reveals his identity as the father of the murderer of Jarvis's son. Kumalo's reply echoes and reechoes the adjective[1]: *It is very heavy, umnumzana. It is the heaviest thing of all my years.... This thing that is the heaviest thing of all my years, is the heaviest thing of all your years also.* Another example occurs early in the novel (25); after Kumalo commends Msimangu's kindness, the latter's demurrer, *I am not kind. I am a selfish and sinful man, but God put his hands on me, that is all,* is echoed by him (215) and by Jarvis at the end of the novel in his last meeting with Kumalo, when the white man *fiercely* interrupts the black pastor's praise by disclaiming any great personal virtue (273):

> —*I am no saintly man, said Jarvis fiercely.*
> —*Of that I cannot speak, but God put His hands on you.*
> *And Jarvis said, That may be, that may be....*

66

Similarly Mrs. Lithebe, whenever she is praised for her great generosity, repeatedly responds with a question that becomes something of a litany: *Why else were we born?*

In their stark simplicity, these and other phrases often suggest the biblical. Like the scripture readings (Chapter 13) and the errant son's name (Absalom), they sometimes even echo the Bible directly, as in this passage (273): Kumalo's *heart went out in great compassion for the boy that must die, who promised now, when there was no more mercy, to sin no more.* Such phrases are so effective because their very understatement heightens the impact of what is clearly implied. They achieve yet greater power because they appear at climactic moments, such as the ones just cited, and they are repeated periodically. Thus their effect also resembles that of the incremental repetition of folk ballads.

Paton's selection of episodes and his narration and descriptions follow a similar stylistic manner. In these, too, understatement and repetition predominate, thus contributing to the desired effect. Almost conspicuously Paton eschews depicting—instead he merely alludes to or presents in the form of newspaper accounts—externally dramatic situations. This is true not only of the most consequential event of the novel—the murder itself—but also of such inherently dramatic situations as the abortive miners' strike or the confrontations between the novel's four sets of fathers and sons: the Kumalos, the Jarvises, the Harrisons, and the Johannesburg Kumalos (John and his son, who represent a different kind of opposition to apartheid).

Instead of depicting violent scenes, Paton interweaves into the narrative events seemingly tangential to the main story line. These events are made interesting in themselves as history, but they are also made immediately pertinent to and revealing of the novel's action and characters. Thus the portrayal of the natives' boycott of the buses (Chapter 8) juxtaposes a vivid picture of this historical event with old Kumalo's search for his son, with Dubula's type of black leadership, and with Msimangu and Kumalo's reactions of some whites' incredible and courageous kindness to the blacks. (Yet another contrast is of course implied in the portrayal of the other black leaders, especially with Kumalo's brother, discussed below.) Similarly, the vignettes of Chapter 9, like John Dos Passos' *U.S.A.* vignettes of the American milieu of the early part of the century, depict the desperate natives' housing shortage and their misery and corruption which accompany the erection of Shanty Town. These vignettes appear as Kumalo prepares to visit his son and the girl in that very Shanty Town, an environment which has already predetermined those young people's wretched existences. In a comparable manner, the discovery of gold in Odendaalsrust (Chapter 23) occurs at the time of Absalom's trial, and it is tied in with the socio-economic realities that, like the treatment of the native miners, have brought and (unless ways are changed) will continue to bring tragedy to blacks and whites alike.

Striking in these descriptions are Paton's changing tone and point of view. Much of the story is seen through the eyes of an omniscient author whose tone ranges from reportorial objectivity to editorial evangelism. Parts of the story, however, are presented through the eyes of one or another of the characters, though this apparently limited point of view is controlled by the author to convey specific effects. Whatever the viewpoint, there are constant yet subtle shifts in tone, ranging from sympathy and hope through bewilderment, grief, and indignation.

The lyrical first paragraph of the brief opening chapter of Book I is identical, word for word, with the opening of Book II: *There is a lovely road that runs from Ixopo into the hills ... which are lovely beyond any singing of it ...* Both openings describe the panoramic beauty and the lush vegetation of the hills. This is the home of Jarvis, and the opening description of Book II, which focuses on Jarvis, stops with the hills. The opening chapter of Book I, which focuses on Kumalo, continues with another and in all respects contrasting description, that of land that is barren and desolate, the valley in which Kumalo and the other blacks live. *The titihoya does not cry here any more,* for here there is insufficient food to attract even a bird. The tone becomes indignant as the green fecundity of the hills is contrasted with the red barrenness of the valley: *Stand shod upon it, for it is coarse and sharp, and the stones cut under the feet. It is not kept, or guarded, or cared for* ... Finally, as we are shown the sterile land in which only the aged are left, the tone becomes elegiac: ... *the young men and the girls are away. The soil cannot keep them any more.*

Even more explicitly 'editorial' are the sections that follow newspaper accounts and such other apparently journalistic digressions as the vignettes on the erection of Shanty Town, the panoramic view of Johannesburg's fear after the murder, and the descriptions of the discovery of gold and the miners' strike. In these chapters' terminal sections, the attitudes implied in the apparently objective narrative are made explicit. After the newspaper report of the murder is read aloud by Father Vincent, for example, his listeners remain silent. But the author editorializes (73 f.): *Sadness and fear and hate, how they well up in the heart and mind, whenever one opens the pages of these messengers of doom. Cry for the broken tribe, for the law and the custom that is gone. Aye, and cry aloud for the man who is dead, for the woman and children bereaved. Cry, the beloved country, these things are not yet at an end. The sun pours down on the earth, on the lovely land that man cannot enjoy. He knows only the fear of his heart.* The chapter immediately following (Chapter 12) presents numerous vignettes (paralleling the vignettes of the misery of Shanty Town in Chapter 9) vivifying the *fear in the land* and the *fear in the heart* that preclude enjoyment of life and the beauty of nature: scenes at a suburban meeting in which are expressed demands for greater police protection, proposals for the amelioration of the natives' poverty and despair, debates on the efficacy (and expense) of educating the blacks, and arguments about enforcing the pass laws; ladies chatting in a country club about various proposals that are unfeasable because they would inconvenience or threaten the whites and are therefore discarded (*Oh, it's too hot to argue. Get your racquet, my dear, they're calling us* ...: 78); and other such settings and discussions. At the conclusion, the author once more editorializes (80): *Cry, the beloved country, for the unborn child that is the inheritor of our fear* ...

Understatement, deceptive simplicity, repetition, selectivity of narrative, episode, and setting, as well as the emotional charge of Paton's style—all these are manifested also in Paton's characterizations.

The novel's major character, the Reverend Stephen Kumalo, has evoked its readers' greatest compassion. Throughout his sufferings he remains an apparently humble, affectionate, kindly, simple, pious, God-fearing old man. Yet far from being simple or simply virtuous, he is portrayed in depth, as a flawed human being. Heroic in his ability to bear terrible private afflictions and tragedy, he is also able to continue to lead his parishioners out of communal suffering and tragedy. At the same time he is subject, too, to anger that manifests itself even in cruelty: to prove her *depravity*, Kumalo viciously tricks his son's mistress into admitting that she *could be willing* to become his own mistress (114); and he frightens his brother by lying, by falsely asserting that John is being observed by spies (211 f.). Kumalo is guilty even of the most heinous of all Christian sins, despair, a sin against which both Msimangu and the kindly English pastor, Father Vincent, sternly caution him on different occasions (89, 108–110). Kumalo is marred, too, by such lesser human flaws as jealousy (when he learns about the salary of the agricultural demonstrator: 251), vanity (his boastful behavior toward fellow blacks in the train to Johannesburg: 13 f.), and pride (in being the brother of a man who enjoys material luxuries: 38); and there is an allusion to an earlier episode that had nearly culminated in adultery with one of his parishioners (270). Finally, though he is well aware of its futility, Kumalo cannot resist repeatedly nagging his already contrite and doomed son with recriminations and unanswerable or futile questions. All these attributes of Kumalo are shown rather than stated, and their manifestations are narrated with striking verbal economy and deceptive simplicity.

Jarvis, Kumalo's white pendant, is more elusively characterized. Seen only after tragedy has struck, Jarvis is never actually shown in his opposition to his son's socio-political beliefs and practices. A single brief speech, however, makes clear that the unportrayed relationship between Jarvis and his son was identical to that of the Harrisons, his daughter-in-law's brother and father. One of their functions in the novel is, precisely, to suggest—without actually depicting—the affectionate yet antagonistic relationship that had existed between Jarvis and his son, Arthur. *My son and I didn't see eye to eye on the native question*, Jarvis tells the younger Harrison; *in fact, he and I got quite heated about it on more than one occasion* (137). But the novel itself depicts only Jarvis's painfully going through his dead son's belongings, agonizing over them, and finally coming to terms not merely with his son's murder (ironically by one of the very natives whose cause he had so fervently championed and whose love he had so widely enjoyed) but with the whole 'native question' and, indeed, with the central 'question' of South Africa—and of universal human brotherhood. His last gesture on that sad visit to Johannesburg is to leave young Harrison a large check with instructions to *do all the things you and Arthur wanted to do* (213).

Even some of the minor characters are portrayed in three-dimensional terms. The almost saintly Msimangu, as he himself says in his already quoted remark, is not flawless; though he later apologizes for his bitter, sarcastic comments to Kumalo about Absalom's girl and her unborn child (68), these comments deeply wounded the already stricken father, as Msimangu knew they were bound to do. His white counterpart, the sympathetic young reformatory worker (who in part personifies Paton himself), later apologizes for his similarly harsh outburst, which also was caused by such frustration, anger, and grief (102–105).

Though less subtle, the characterization of Kumalo's brother is striking. Both John's private and his public actions (especially in Chapter 26, which shows him on the speaker's platform, mesmerizing even his brother and worrying the white constabulary) help to develop his portrayal as a very great orator with the voice of a bull (and other bullish attributes) who could rally the natives to revolution in order to assert their human rights. But he stops short of the decisive step because he is a cowardly opportunist out only to get what he can in a society structured to keep him enslaved, and he is too amoral and—above all—too fearful of jeopardizing his personal comfort and success. *There is no applause in prison*, the omniscient author wryly observes (186), and Msimangu expresses his relief at John's corruption, *for if he were not corrupt, he could plunge this country into bloodshed. He is corrupted by his possessions, and he fears their loss, and the loss of the power he already has* (187). How right Msimangu is in this assessment is clearly shown in the brief description of John's immediate panicky reaction to his brother's suggestion that he might be arrested: *The big bull man wiped the sweat from his brow* (211). His deficient leadership is thus explicitly contrasted with that of Dubula and Tomlinson, especially as depicted in Dubula's participation in the bus boycott scene (Chapter 8).

In a comparable manner, their sister, Gertrude, another minor character, is also presented meaningfully. She is believable as a decent woman driven to brassy whoredom and shabby motherhood by apartheid and its effects. But she strives for decency, however unsuccessfully, escaping her tormenting fleshly temptations only by joining a nunnery. In contrast, Absalom's mistress, despite a similar past, fits into Kumalo's pious life style as soon as she enters Mrs. Lithebe's house. *The girl is not like Gertrude. She is openly glad to be in this house*, the narrator says, and Mrs. Lithebe does not need to chide her as she must chide Gertrude (119 f.). Such carefully and subtly and symmetrically wrought contrasts are achieved in the portrayals of these women just as they are in the portrayals of the Kumalo brothers, of Jarvis, and of Harrison—all members of the conflicting old order as well as fathers in conflict with their sons, proponents of differing new moral as well as new social orders.

Note

1. Alan Paton, *Cry, the Beloved Country*, New York (Charles Scribner's Sons) 1948, 180. Quotations from the novel are from this edition.

ROBERT L. DUNCAN ON THE SUFFERING SERVANT

"By common consent," writes C.R. North, the author of a definitive study of the Suffering Servant, Isaiah 52:13–53:12 is the "most important" and the "most discussed passage in the O.T."[1] It is the fourth and longest of four "Servant Songs" in Isaiah that portray a mysterious figure whose vicarious sufferings will be the means of redeeming mankind.[2] "Perhaps no other problem in the Hebrew Bible," ventures Abraham J. Heschel, "has occupied the minds of scholars more than the identification and interpretation of the servant."[3] If Isaiah 53 has been provocative to biblical scholars seeking to identify the Suffering Servant, it has also been provocative to writers seeking to dramatize and make sense of the chaos of the modern world. (...)

Perhaps what has especially attracted these writers to Isaiah 53 is the panorama of anguish and pain borne by the Servant as portrayed in the passage. North identifies five strophes in this poem and points out that strophe 3 (53:4–6) is especially striking in that it "gives the impression that the Servant was subjected to every conceivable pain and indignity."[4] Indeed, the entire poem offers a comprehensive vision of human misery. The Servant is identified with all the mental, emotional, and physical pain to which human beings are subject. He voluntarily identifies himself with this wretchedness because the Lord has called him to vicarious suffering to bring about divine forgiveness, healing, and reconciliation for mankind (53:10–12; cf. vss. 4–6). (...)

Alan Paton directly quotes verses (Isa. 42:6–7) from the immediate context of the first Servant Song (Isa. 42:1–4) to define the redemptive role of the Christian when confronted by suffering. (Indeed, in the view of some scholars these verses belong to that poem.) He also quotes these same verses in an essay setting forth this view of the nature of the Christian community. Moreover, the novel provides imagery and symbolism, as well as conceptions of the meaning of suffering, that reflect the main ideas of Isaiah 53 and other Servant poems.

The enduring significance of Paton's novel lies not only in its treatment of the suffering engendered by apartheid in South Africa, but also in its presentation of human suffering in the broad picture, the comprehensive human misery revealed in the Suffering Servant text of Isaiah 53. Moreover, it presents a response to such suffering that reflects the restorative and reconciling role of the Suffering Servant, and the creation, as in the Christian interpretation of the Servant phenomenon, of a community that emulates the Servant's compassionate identification with human pain (cf. I Pet. 2:21–25).

The novel is the story of a black Anglican priest, Stephen Kumalo, whose son, Absalom, leaves home, as do so many young blacks in South Africa, and journeys to Johannesburg. Alienated from his son geographically, but also, like the biblical David and his son of the same name, emotionally and spiritually, the Reverend Kumalo travels to the city in search of Absalom, only to discover that he has been involved with two other young blacks in a robbery and murder. The victim is Arthur Jarvis, coincidentally the son of James Jarvis, a prosperous farmer whose farm lies not far from Ndotsheni, where Stephen Kumalo's church is located. As a result of Arthur's murder, James Jarvis, too, sets out on a "search" for his son as he seeks to understand Arthur's deep commitment to social justice for the South African natives. Much suffering results from these events, including suffering that is traceable to apartheid and its consequences, but also suffering that results from the general human condition: parents lose their sons, wives and children are bereaved of husbands and fathers, oppressed people are victimized by social and political systems, brothers and sisters are alienated from each other because of differing life styles and values, a husband loses his wife to illness, individuals have their suffering compounded because of the thoughtlessness and cruelty of others. And one could go on.

But the novel offers a redemptive response to this suffering. Thus, as Stephen Kumalo searches for Absalom in Book I, he is sustained in his suffering by various people, especially

Msimangu, a young black priest. And James Jarvis's search for his son in Book II leads to a sympathy with Arthur's commitment to social justice that compels him to alleviate the suffering of the blacks at Ndotsheni. Thus, Book III may be termed the Book of Restoration[11] because it tells of the reconciliation, through their mutual suffering and compassion, of Jarvis and Kumalo, and the beginning of the restoration of the eroded and arid native land around Ndotsheni and of the Reverend Kumalo's church through the moral commitment and financial backing of James Jarvis. The novel, however, ends on an uncertain note of hope mingled with deep grief as Stephen Kumalo somberly observes the moment of his son's execution.

Although Stephen Kumalo experiences the warmth and support of the Christian community soon after his arrival in Johannesburg, it is the subsequent death of Arthur Jarvis that connects the deep despair in the first part of the novel with the reconciliation and restoration of the last part. His death thus has a redemptive value, which is underscored by his father's eucharistic-like remark that he and his wife performed their deeds of restoration "in memory of our beloved son" (p. 262). Yet his murder appears absurd and meaningless. He merely happened to be at home with a "slight cold" on the day of the robbery and thus heard the noise of the intruders. At that very moment he was working on a manuscript titled "The Truth About Native Crime" in which he was arguing that white suppression of the blacks was responsible for black crime. His life, as his father learned from his papers, was wholly dedicated to the cause of justice for the natives. Yet, he is killed by a frightened young black who has drifted into the criminal behavior typical of the natives who, compelled to leave their homes because the land allotted to their people by the white-controlled government will not support them, migrate to Johannesburg only to become corrupted by the deleterious influence of the city. Paradoxically, it is this absurd situation that leads to the reconciliation and restoration occurring in the latter part of the novel.

In Msimangu's sermon to the blind at Ezenzelini, a sermon

that serves temporarily to lift Stephen Kumalo out of the despair into which he has sunk at the news of the murder, he quotes Isaiah 42:16, a chapter in which the first of the four Servant poems appears (p. 90). One line reads, "I will make darkness light before them," thus suggesting the emergence of light from darkness. This imagery occurs often in the first three Servant poems and related passages and corresponds to the pattern of the fourth, as salvation emerges from the suffering of the Servant.[12] It also provides the pattern for suffering and redemption in *Cry, the Beloved Country*.

Thus, for example, on the evening following his return to Ndotsheni, Stephen Kumalo converses with an old friend on human suffering and concludes: "I believe but I have learned that it is a secret. Pain and suffering, they are a secret. Kindness and love, they are a secret. But I have learned," he observes, almost in terms of atonement, "that kindness and love can pay for pain and suffering." His friend responds that Christ suffered, "not to save us from suffering, but *to teach us how to bear suffering* [emphasis mine]." Thus the revelatory light of kindness and love emerges as a "secret," a divine mystery, from the darkness of suffering when Christians, like the Servant, learn how to bear pain, their own and that of others. As the darkness of evening advances, Kumalo decides to let the lamp burn longer than usual: "Let it burn for what has happened here," he says to his wife, referring to the joy and love with which the Christian community has welcomed him home, but, he adds, "let it be put out for what has happened otherwise" (pp. 226–28). In the theology of *Cry, the Beloved Country*, therefore, redemptive love and suffering are bound together, the one emerging from the other and "making darkness light."

Near the end of the novel, as James Jarvis and Stephen Kumalo meet for the last time, Jarvis, seeking to console Kumalo over the approaching execution of his son, speaks of his plans for the restoration of the valley and the church. When Kumalo seeks to thank him, he responds, "I have seen a man ... who was in *darkness* [emphasis mine] till you found him. If that is what you do, I give it willingly" (p. 272). Jarvis, too, has passed from the "darkness" of grief and blindness to the plight of the blacks, to the "light" of dynamic concern, in this case, through the compassionate witness of Kumalo, who himself has emerged from the darkness of suffering and paralyzing doubt to the light of renewed faith, hope, and love.

Out of the "darkness" of suffering triggered by the murder, therefore, emerges the "light" of reconciliation and restoration in Book III of the novel. And as the Servant dies vicariously for those who do not understand his mission, so Arthur Jarvis is murdered by the very people to whose welfare he has dedicated his life and talents. Also, like the Servant, he offers himself without resistance: the newspaper report of the robbery and murder states that "there were no signs of any struggle" (p. 73). Arthur Jarvis had just written lines that argued white responsibility for native crime. How, then, could he use violence against the native intruders?

The result of this "vicarious" death is the creation of a Servant community made up of those people, including Mrs. Lithebe, Father Vincent, Msimangu, and James Jarvis, who become compassionate agents of restoration. Although this community, with the exception of Jarvis, sustained Stephen Kumalo before the murder, it is galvanized to a greater dimension of redemptive compassion and support for Kumalo by the unbearable anguish that he experiences upon learning that his son is the murderer of Arthur Jarvis. As in the example of Jesus the Servant, this identification with suffering is the manifestation, not of a masochism, but of self-giving compassion. As Paton has written in an article titled "Toward a Spiritual Community," Christianity "meets suffering, not with stoicism or resignation, but with compassion...." In this context, Paton cites Isaiah 42:6–7, a passage Msimangu quotes in his sermon to the blind: "I the Lord have called thee in righteousness, to open the blind eyes, to bring the prisoners out of the prison, and them that sit in *darkness* [emphasis mine] out of the prisonhouse."[13] Paton's title for this article, his comments on Christian compassion, and his citation of the passage from Isaiah illustrate how Christian suffering and the creation of the spiritual community are linked in his thought and how both are rooted in the Servant theology of the prophet.

James Jarvis's search for the meaning of his son's life and death eventually leads him to Arthur's study and the pictures, books, and papers there, especially the speeches and articles written by his son. Two of the four pictures on the wall are of Christ crucified and Abraham Lincoln, both of whom suffered vicariously and died redemptively. Jarvis "looked long" at these pictures. When he later returns to his son's study, he again looks at these pictures. And later still, having escaped with Kumalo from a rainstorm into the leaky and ramshackle church of Ndotsheni, he expressed his compassionate understanding of what it means to Kumalo that his son is to die and looks "towards the altar and the cross on the altar." In the study, he selects a book of Lincoln's speeches and reads the Gettysburg Address, "apparently a speech that was a failure, but that had since become one of the great speeches of the world." Thus, through the pictures of the suffering Christ and the martyred Lincoln, as well as the altar, the cross, and the speech, one is reminded of how profound values and benefits may emerge from apparent failure, the pattern of the darkness–light motif in the novel and of the Servant Songs.

As pointed out by Stephen Kumalo's old friend, Christ suffered to teach his people "how to bear suffering." Father Vincent, a white Anglican priest, also speaks of the role of Christ in human suffering in response to Kumalo's attempt to thank him for his compassion: "We do what is in us, and why it is in us that is also a secret. It is Christ in us, crying that men may be succoured and forgiven, even when He Himself is forsaken" (p. 110). In his priestly admonishment to the Reverend Kumalo, Father Vincent uses "secret" five times, thus stressing the mystery of God's work of redemptive compassion in the world and the consequent necessity of faith. The redemptive work of God in the Suffering Servant is also a "secret" because it is so contrary to human understanding and expectations: "Who has believed what we have heard? And to whom has the arm of the Lord been revealed? ... He was despised and rejected by men ... we esteemed him not ... we esteemed him stricken, smitten by God, and afflicted" (53:1, 3, 4). The forsakeness and suffering of Christ the Servant are offered by Father Vincent as the reason why his people reach out in compassion to give comfort and forgiveness to others who suffer.

The role of Christ in human compassion toward suffering and the darkness–light motif are also connected in the redemptive reflections of Stephen Kumalo on Msimangu's sermon to the blind: "Who gives, at this one hour, a friend to make darkness light before me? .... If Christ be Christ, he says, true Lord of Heaven, true Lord of Men, what is there that we would not do no matter what our suffering may be?" (p. 91). This passage also points up that the identification of the Servant community with suffering is both a matter of shared suffering and compassionate service, as Paton stresses in his essay "Toward the Spiritual Community," cited above.

Thus, in the Suffering Servant theology of *Cry, the Beloved Country* it is God who brings the light of reconciliation and restoration out of the darkness of the death of Arthur Jarvis and who, through the suffering of his Servant-Son, creates the Servant Community from those who suffer because of this tragedy and those who compassionately identify with their suffering. That this fictional vision represents the author's view is confirmed by Paton's answer in an essay to his own question of what the Christian should do who is confronted by suffering and injustice in a society that is hostile to efforts to alleviate these conditions: "There is only one answer for the Christian who has come, often reluctantly, often fearfully, to the belief that the cross is not just for Good Friday. He must do it if he can."[14] Thus, Paton directly links the Christian's duty to bear the burdens of the anguished and oppressed with the suffering of Christ the Servant upon the cross (cf. Lk. 9:23).

Notes

1. *Isaiah 40–55: The Suffering Servant of God* (London: SCM Press, 1952), p. 130.

2. Although there are scholarly variations as to the precise boundaries of the Suffering Servant poems, the following passages, in addition to 52:13–53:12, are usually so designated: 42:1–4; 49:1–6; 50:4–11. Many Old Testament scholars argue that Isaiah 40–55 was not written by Isaiah

of the eighth century B.C. but by an unknown prophet writing toward the end of the Exile. He is often termed Deutero- or Second-Isaiah. There are, however, conservative scholars who maintain the unity of Isaiah. My argument is unaffected by this difference, except in the references to the Babylonian Captivity as the prophet's milieu.

3. *The Prophets* (New York: Harper & Row, 1962), p. 149 note.

4. *Isaiah 40–55*, pp. 130, 135.

11. Edward Callan, *Alan Paton*, rev. edn. (Boston: Twayne Publishers, 1982), p. 39.

12. Msimangu also quotes Isaiah 42:6–7, where the prophet speaks of the Servant as a light-bearer to the Gentiles who will release from prison those who "sit in darkness." See also 42:3; 49:6, 8–9, 50:10–11.

13. "Toward a Spiritual Community." *Christian Century*, March 8, 1950, p. 299.

14. "The Problem of Evil," in *Alan Paton: Knocking on the Door*, ed. Colin Gardner (New York: Charles Scribner's Sons, 1975), p. 216.

J.M. COETZEE ON SIMPLE LANGUAGE

In Alan Paton's *Cry, the Beloved Country* (1948), the Reverend Stephen Kumalo, whose son is charged with murdering a white man, is told that a prominent advocate will appear for the defence *pro deo*. How can he afford an advocate's fees, Kumalo asks. His friend replies:

—Did you not hear him say he would take the case pro deo? ... It is Latin, and it means for God. So it will cost you nothing, or at least very little.
—He takes it for God?
—That is what it meant in the old days of faith, though it has lost much of that meaning. But it still means that the case is taken for nothing. [125]

Kumalo's friend is partly right, partly wrong. The words *pro deo* used to mean, and still mean, "for God." In a legal context, however, they mean "without payment." The information about God is interesting historical background, but it carries as little semantic weight as the information that *martial* once contained a reference to Mars. Words do not bear their histories with them as part of their meaning.

Elsewhere in Paton's novel, Kumalo—a country priest on his first visit to Johannesburg—has gold mining explained to him by a fellow-Zulu:

> We go down and dig it [the ore] out, umfundisi [sir]. And when it is hard to dig, we go away, and the white men blow it out with the fire-sticks. Then ... we load it on to the trucks, and it goes up in a cage, up a long chimney so long that I cannot say it for you. [16]

Just as the (English) speech of Pauline Smith's Afrikaans characters is marked for Afrikaans origin, the speech of Kumalo's informant here is marked for Zulu origin, not only by the transcription of Zulu words like *umfundisi* but by words like *fire-sticks* (i.e., dynamite), *chimney* (i.e., shaft), and *go away* (i.e., take cover), as well as by an ungrammatical use of the English definite article ("the fire-sticks"). The reader cannot be blamed for concluding that Zulu lacks words for the concepts *dynamite, shaft, take cover*, that the speaker is using the best approximations his language provides, and that Paton has given literal translations of these approximations, in accord with the practice of transfer.

In fact this conclusion is false. The Zulu for mine shaft is *umgodi*, a word quite distinct from *ushimula* (chimney), whose English origin is clear. The word for dynamite, again of English origin, is *udalimede*, which has nothing to do with fire-sticks. *Banda* (to take cover) is clearly distinguished from *suka* (to go away).

Thus while Paton uses the same principle as Smith, his practice has a shakier linguistic foundation. Smith's Afrikaans transfers are based on a more or less accurate, if limited, knowledge of Afrikaans. Paton, on the other hand, is content to create the *impression* that a transfer from Zulu has taken place. We see the trick most clearly in the phrase "the fire-sticks." Zulu speakers speaking English often have difficulty with the English article, since Zulu has no corresponding lexical form.

But it is of course a mistake to conclude that Zulu speakers cannot make the semantic distinctions for which English relies on the article. "The fire-sticks" merely reproduces a common mistake made by Zulus speaking English; it says nothing about Zulus speaking Zulu.

The overt purpose of transfer is to make the reader imagine the words he is reading have a foreign original behind them. The artificial literalism of passages like the above, however, conveys in addition a certain naiveté, even childishness, which reflects on the quality of mind of its speaker and of Zulu speakers in general.

One of the more poignant conversations in the novel takes place—in Zulu, we are told—between Kumalo and James Jarvis, the father of the man whom Kumalo's son has killed. The two meet by accident. Jarvis, who does not yet know of the tragic connection between them, speaks:

> —You are in fear of me, but I do not know what it is. You need not be in fear of me.
> —It is true, umnumzana [sir]. You do not know what it is.
> —I do not know but I desire to know.
> —I doubt if I could tell it, umnumzana. You must tell it, umfundisi. Is it heavy?
> —It is very heavy, umnumzana. It is the heaviest thing in all my years. [180]

What motive can Paton have for writing *be in fear of* instead of *be afraid of*, *desire* instead of *would like*, *heavy* instead of *serious*? In each case the synonyms translate the same putative Zulu original. In each case the choice is stylistic. The first member of each pair has a touch of archaism; this archaism makes for a certain ceremoniousness in the verbal exchanges, whose effect it is to hold any unseemly display of emotion at bay (the sentimentality of *Cry, the Beloved Country* is largely a matter of ostentatious stoicism of this kind). But the archaism of the English implies something else too: an archaic quality to the Zulu behind it, as if the Zulu language, Zulu culture, the Zulu frame of mind, belonged to a bygone and heroic age.

The Zulu original implied by Paton's English is both unrelievedly simple—there is a minimum of syntactic embedding—and formal to the point of stateliness. In its closeness to its historical roots, in its preference for parable over abstraction (Paton explicitly compares it to the "symbolic language" of parable [108]), Zulu—Paton's Zulu—seems to belong to an earlier and more innocent era in human culture. From the fact that Kumalo's politician brother prefers to use English, the reader may further surmise that Zulu is as inhospitable to lies and deception as it is to complexity and abstraction.

The phantom Zulu of *Cry, the Beloved Country* is in fact less the medium through which Paton's characters speak than part of the interpretation Paton wishes us to make of them. It tells us that they belong in an old-fashioned context of direct (i.e., unmediated) personal relations based on respect, obedience, and fidelity. These values are epitomised in an episode towards the end of the book. Jarvis has begun to send a daily gift of milk to the children of Kumalo's village. The man who brings the milk tells Kumalo: "I have worked only a week there [at Jarvis's farm], but the day he says to me, die, I shall die" (238). Self-sacrificial loyalty of this kind won for the Zulus the admiration of Victorian England; it is clearly a virtue Paton approves of. But these words also give us to understand that, by his receptivity to "Zulu" speech and his "Zulu" qualities, Jarvis has crossed the barrier between white and black and taken the place of the chief in his servant's heart.

What, if anything, then, separates Paton from those writers of the 1930s and 1940s who, under one disguise or another, call for the movement of history to come to a halt, for economic, social, and personal relations in the South African countryside to freeze forever in feudal postures? The answer is that, with however much regret, Paton accepts that the economic, and hence the political, basis of feudalism has been eroded by demographic forces. Kumalo's aspiration, in the wake of his son's death, is to hold together the remnants of his community in a muted version of black pastoral. But for how long? The fact is that the exhausted soil can no longer support them. As the young agricultural expert tells him, "We can restore this valley for those who are here, but when the children grow up, there will again be too many" (268). To this young man Paton allots the last and most telling word. To his logic Kumalo and his patron Jarvis, with their fragile hope of preserving an Eden in the valley immune from the attractions of the great city, have no response.

Tony Adler on *Cry, the Beloved Country* and *Lost in the Stars*

Published in 1948 but cast in a high, pure, poetic direction that echoes the Bible, the *Odyssey* of Homer, the voices found in stories that were spoken long before they were written down, *Cry, the Beloved Country* offers its tragic vision of life under apartheid without resort to the modern tics of cynicism or facile irony. The tone is grave. The manner is spare and deliberate—almost naively so, as if the author knew he was describing something so deep and complex, so delicate and momentous that only the most careful construction of the most careful words would serve; as if he knew that a single moment's retreat from clarity would reduce the book and its vision to the murderous chaos from which he was trying so hard to save it.

"The story is mythic," says [Frank] Galati [author of a stage version of the novel, performed at the Goodman Theatre in Chicago in June 1993]. "The story has hidden lessons in it. It is deeply layered, so the voicing of the story has the ring of a sage, a poet, a bard, a rhapsode, a chronicler of a people."

In 1948 the American playwright Maxwell Anderson bought the stage rights for *Cry, the Beloved Country* and, together with the legendary German emigré composer Kurt Weill, built a "musical tragedy" around it. Titled *Lost in the Stars*, the Anderson/Weill adaptation tells basically the same story Paton tells: that of an old black country parson named Stephen Kumalo who searches the city of Johannesburg for his wayward son, Absalom, only to see him arrested for having shot a young white man to death in the course of a bungled burglary.

But telling basically the same story isn't necessarily the same thing as telling essentially the same story. *Lost in the Stars* and *Cry, the Beloved Country* diverge not only in some basics, but in their essences as well.

Galati found this out as soon as he began working on Anderson's script in preparation for what he initially thought would be a Goodman revival of *Lost in the Stars*. "You see when you read the play how widely Anderson diverged from the novel," he says. "There may be a few fragments of dialogue that are from the novel, but even the dialogue and the speeches, the rhetoric, the text itself is all Maxwell Anderson's invention."

Understanding apartheid

Anderson and Weill ditched the bardic gravity of the novel's voice in favor of something harder, livelier and more profane: something closer to the voice one finds in Weill's most famous collaboration—the one with Bertolt Brecht, on *The Threepenny Opera*. They dropped certain significant characters and reduced others to sentimental cartoons, reflecting the liberal cliches of the time.

Where, for instance, Jarvis, the father of the murdered white man, goes through an extraordinarily delicate transformation in the novel, coming to understand his dead son's anti-apartheid politics as a consequence of coming to understand his son, Anderson and Weill turn him into a stiff-necked bigot whose conversion, when it finally happens, is about as subtle—and dramatically motivated—as Saint Paul getting blasted by a bolt of lightening.

Stephen Kumalo comes in for similarly rough treatment. Not only is Paton's modest, almost excruciatingly private little parson remade by Anderson and Weill into a soulful bass baritone à la Paul Robeson, he's also the victim of the most maudlin sort of liberal condescension. In an oafish rewriting of his encounter with Jarvis, Kumalo is made to beg the white man for mercy—something he does not even so much as contemplate doing in the book.

The effect is to denigrate Stephen Kumalo's dignity, his tragedy, his heartfelt Christian values—and to supplant him as the moral focus of the drama. What had been the tale of one black man's trek through a South African valley of the shadow becomes the story of his redemption at the hands of a beneficent white guy. (...)

Restoring a masterpiece

"It's an unbelievable inversion of the whole moral center of the story!" sputters the normally gracious Galati, in an uncharacteristic burst of exasperation.

But even more profound than the difference between the Paton and Anderson/Weill visions of Kumalo is the difference between their visions of the universe itself.

Alan Paton was heartbroken by the treatment that this character and his story received at the hands of Anderson and Weill," says Galati. "He said his little parson would never have sung a song like 'Lost in the Stars.' He wasn't lost in the stars. What Paton objected to was the application of a kind of existential godlessness, a faithlessness that permeates the world of the play: Here we are, out lost in the stars....

> "The idea is anathema to Paton, whose novel is all about faith and a deep commitment to fundamental human goodness in the face of insurmountable obstacles: evil, fear, degeneracy, violence, and the corroding and corrupting impact of, for instance, liquor and prostitution, child abuse and abandonment and slavery. I mean, there's rage in the novel insofar as rage is a perfectly understandable reaction to the terrible pain and deprivation and inequality of the social structure in South Africa. But above all and transcending the rage, there is faith. The novel is a novel in which there is God."

CAROL IANNONE ON PATON'S TRAGIC LIBERALISM

In an essay written in 1975, Nadine Gordimer declared that South African literature in English had "made a new beginning with Alan Paton's *Cry, the Beloved Country*, and indeed it could be said that Paton's novel put South Africa on the twentieth-century literary map. Within a few years of its publication in 1948, it had become a worldwide best-seller and was eventually translated into twenty, languages. At the time of Paton's death in 1988, it had sold over fifteen million copies and was still selling at the rate of one hundred thousand copies a year. It is not solely in literary terms that a South African novel of the twentieth century must make its mark, however, and Gordimer went on to say that Paton's "was a book of lyrical beauty and power that moved the conscience of the outside world over racialism and, what's more, that of white South Africa as no book had done before." (...)

In later years, Paton often observed that South Africa had very little to unite it—what with myriad African tribes, a population of Indians and "coloreds," and two different white "races," all with separate languages, cultures, histories, values, and symbols. South Africa's union had been brought about by war and politics more than by shared ideals. Only the physical land itself might inspire common loyalty. As Maxwell Perkins observed, the land is one of the chief characters in *Cry, the Beloved Country*. The novel opens with a lyrical description of the spectacular landscape of the Ixopo district in Natal:

> There is a lovely road that runs from Ixopo into the hills. These hills are grass-covered and rolling, and they are lovely beyond any singing of it. The road climbs seven miles into them, to Carisbrooke; and from there, if there is no mist, you look down on one of the fairest valleys of Africa. About you there is grass and bracken and you may hear the forlorn crying of the titihoya, one of the birds of the veld. Below you is the valley of the Umzimkulu, on its journey from the Drakensberg to the sea; and beyond and behind the river, great hill after great hill; and beyond and behind them, the mountains of Ingeli and East Griqualand.
> The grass is rich and matted, you cannot see the soil. It holds the rain and the mist, and they seep into the

ground, feeding the streams in every kloof. It is well-tended, and not too many cattle feed upon it; not too many fires burn it, laying bare the soil. Stand unshod upon it, for the ground is holy, being even as it came from the Creator.

The narrative then shifts to a very different terrain, one that reflects the division in the society itself:

Where you stand the grass is rich and matted, you cannot see the soil. But the rich green hills break down. They fall to the valley below, and falling, change their nature. For they grow red and bare; they cannot hold the rain and mist, and the streams are dry in the kloofs. Too many cattle feed upon the grass, and too many fires have burned it. Stand shod upon it, for it is coarse and sharp, and the stones cut under the feet. It is not kept, or guarded, or cared for, it no longer keeps men, guards men, cares for men. The titihoya does not cry here any more.

The great red hills stand desolate, and the earth has torn away like flesh. The lightning flashes over them, the clouds pour down upon them, the dead streams come to life, full of the red blood of the earth. Down in the valleys women scratch the soil that is left, and the maize hardly reaches the height of a man. They are valleys of old men and old women, of mothers and children. The men are away, the young men and the girls are away. The soil cannot keep them any more.

This poorer district is named Ndotsheni by the author. The action begins when the main character, Stephen Kumalo, a devout Zulu parson of an impoverished rural Anglican parish, receives a letter from a stranger summoning him to Johannesburg. According to the letter, Kumalo's much younger sister Gertrude is in need. Gertrude went to the big city with her small son some time before to find her husband who had gone to work in the gold mines. Kumalo's son Absalom is also in the city; he went to look for Gertrude and has lost touch with his old parents. Once Kumalo arrives in Johannesburg, he is helped by a group of Anglican priests, both black and white, who minister in a black slum called Sophiatown.

Kumalo finds his family drastically changed. His brother John, who moved to the city some years before, is living with a woman not his wife and has become a racial militant, full of the germinating anger of the de-tribalized, de-Christianized, urbanized South Africa that Paton saw waiting in the wings. Moreover, Kumalo learns with sorrow that his sister Gertrude has sunk into prostitution and that, during the very course of Kumalo's desperate search for him, Absalom has committed murder while breaking into a house with two companions.

Meanwhile, James Jarvis, a wealthy English-speaking farmer from the fertile area described in the opening passages, has learned that his grown son Arthur has been shot to death in his home in Johannesburg. The elder Jarvis and his wife must also journey to the city for the funeral and trial. There he learns from the police what has since brought Stephen Kumalo almost to the breaking point, that Absalom Kumalo is the killer of his son. Thus the two worlds collide.

A later critic faulted Paton for not giving Absalom's point of view, but the novel works from the standpoint of the older generation. As the two fathers struggle to understand what has become of their sons, the anguish of the beloved country unfolds. "When people go to Johannesburg they don't come back," murmurs Kumalo's wife, Grace. Absalom fell in with "bad companions," one of them his own cousin Matthew, John's son, but Kumalo remains aghast at how his well brought up boy could have committed so terrible a deed. For his part, Jarvis too will learn more about a side of his son that he barely knew. Arthur had been president of the African Boys Club and a proponent of racial reform, so his death at the hands of a young native seems ironic. Among Arthur's effects Jarvis finds manuscripts and articles through which he learns, painfully and in detail, about his son's strongly held racial views. At the funeral, which is attended by all shades and colors of people, Jarvis finds himself shaking black hands for the first time in his life.

The novel's success may have been due, in part, to the moment of South African history that it captured, 1946, before the imposition of "grand apartheid" was to consume the country completely in politics. The depression and war had passed. Industrialization and urbanization were breaking down tribal customs, even as the increasing population of blacks and whites in the cities was worsening the tensions under separatism. The novel strips away the surface assurances of white supremacy to reveal what has in some respects become a wasteland—a literal wasteland in the case of the sordid slums and the dying tribal lands, but also a spiritual wasteland, characterized by alienation and mistrust among races and peoples and families and generations. "It is fear that rules this land," says Msimangu, one of the black priests who helps Kumalo.

So painful is the reality depicted in *Cry, the Beloved Country* that when the playwright Maxwell Anderson adapted the novel for the stage (with music by Kurt Weill), he called it *Lost in the Stars*, and made it a cry against a God who had abandoned his creatures. This was done much to Paton's consternation. His perspective is thoroughly Christian, though in the sense of a struggle for the light, not in the application of received truths. The novel manifests both Christian and tragic qualities. The final answers are "secrets" and "mysteries" that reside only with God, and at any given moment the divine may not be evident or clear. The characters must bear up in the face of desolation, injustice, pain, and loss, but there is also hope, comfort, and consolation.

Thus despite the good liberal intentions behind the novel to move white South Africans over conditions in their society, *Cry, the Beloved Country* does not evidence the kind of superficiality that Lionel Trilling felt was typical of what he called "the liberal imagination." Avoiding easy answers, Paton enters into the perspective of both "victims" and "oppressors," and demonstrates a humility and acceptance before the unknown and unresolvable.

Both the 1995 film version (starring James Earl Jones) and the Anderson play evince the thinner imaginative capacity of much contemporary liberalism and thus provide an instructive contrast to Paton's greater subtlety. In the film, worthy on many other counts, the delicacy that Paton achieved in portraying Jarvis's racialism is partly destroyed by the drive toward ideological simplification. In the film, James Jarvis refers to blacks as kaffirs, an insulting word that is out of character for the Jarvis of the novel. Even more untrue to Paton's vision, the Jarvis in the film refuses to shake the black hand that is proffered to him at his son's funeral. In an even greater departure from Paton, the Jarvis figure in the Maxwell Anderson adaptation is an out-and-out white supremacist spouting forth on the necessity for the white man to dominate the black. But Paton knew that South Africa's problem lay as much in the softer, unarticulated sort of racialism as in the ideological kind.

The 1951 film, directed by Zoltan Korda and written by Paton, with Sidney Poitier as Msimangu, is faithful to Paton's nuanced tragic vision. Although it might be too low-key for some tastes and was not commercially successful ("When does your film start?" asked Alexander Korda, Zoltan's brother, at an early screening), it is deeply moving, especially for those who know the novel.

Paton's rejection of easy racial moralism does not mean that he exonerates the South African system. Far from it. But he doesn't go in for the blanket indictment of South Africa that became typical in later years. Msimangu castigates the white man for giving "too little ... almost nothing" to the blacks, but he also acknowledges the gift of Christianity and appreciates the good white people who do what they can. On the other side, the fiery speech of John Kumalo demanding higher wages makes a lot of sense, notwithstanding the menacing anger that informs it.

In one of Arthur's writings, a work in progress discovered by his father after his death, Paton provides a lengthy version of his own thought, though skillfully tailored to reflect Arthur's younger, more naive understanding. Arthur carefully distinguishes what was "permissible" from what was "not permissible" in South Africa's history. Reflecting an earlier understanding of colonialism, he does not feel it necessary to delegitimize all of white South Africa:

What we did when we came to South Africa was permissible. It was permissible to develop the great resources with the aid of what labour we could find. It was permissible to use unskilled men for unskilled work. But it is not permissible to keep men unskilled for the sake of unskilled work.

It was permissible when we discovered gold to bring labour to the mines. It was permissible to build compounds and to keep women and children away from the towns. It was permissible as an experiment, in the light of what we knew. But in the light of what we know now, with certain exceptions, it is no longer permissible. It is not permissible for us to go on destroying family life when we know that we are destroying it.

This aspect of the novel has perhaps not been fully appreciated. Paton had a tragic grasp of the way good and evil are interwoven in human history. In Arthur Jarvis he created a character who understood the inevitability of civilizational progress and expansion and the conflict and loss that they bring. At the same time, Arthur insists that the colonizers take responsibility for the damage they have done in the process:

> The old tribal system was, for all its violence and savagery, for all its superstition and witchcraft, a moral system. Our natives today produce criminals and prostitutes and drunkards, not because it is their nature to do so, but because their simple system of order and tradition and convention has been destroyed. It was destroyed by the impact of our own civilization. Our civilization has therefore an inescapable duty to set up another system of order and tradition and convention.

Knowing that South Africa prides itself on being a Christian nation, Arthur reproaches it for its hypocrisy, and, by the by, renders a shrewd analysis of the psychology of racism:

The truth is that our Christian civilization is riddled through and through with dilemma. We believe in the brotherhood of man, but we do not want it in South Africa. We believe that God endows men with diverse gifts, and that human life depends for its fullness on their employment and enjoyment, but we are afraid to explore this belief too deeply.... We say we withhold education because the black child has not the intelligence to profit by it; we withhold opportunity because black people have no gifts.... We shift our ground again when a black man does achieve something remarkable, and feel deep pity for a man who is condemned to the loneliness of being remarkable, and decide that it is a Christian kindness not to let black men become remarkable. Thus even our God becomes a confused and inconsistent creature, giving gifts and denying them employment.... The truth is that our civilization is not Christian; it is a tragic compound of great ideal and fearful practice, of high assurance and desperate anxiety, of loving charity and fearful clutching of possessions.

These are nearly the last words that Arthur wrote before his murder.

As bad as social conditions are for blacks, however, they do not entirely explain the senseless murder of a son, husband, and father, and a man "devoted to our people." There were those who had tried to help Absalom. He had spent time in a Diepkloof-like reformatory, where a young official obtained a job for him and arranged for his release so that he might assume responsibility for the girl he had made pregnant. But such aid could not overcome the temptations and confusions Absalom faced in the big city.

At the trial, the judge acknowledges and perhaps even partly concedes the arguments by Absalom's lawyer regarding the "disastrous effect" of tribal breakdown that the victim Arthur Jarvis himself wrote about. But, the judge asserts, "even if it be true that we have, out of fear and selfishness and thoughtlessness, wrought a destruction that we have done little to repair ... a Judge may not trifle with the Law because the society is defective.... Under the law a man is held responsible for his deeds."

Under South African law, a conviction of murder requires that "an intention to kill" be established. Absalom's lawyer argues that the young man did not mean to kill but only fired his gun out of fear. The judge finds an intention by "inference" in Absalom's carrying a loaded gun while breaking into a home. In ruling so, the judge is applying a standard of legal responsibility and conscious deliberation where conditions of social disorder and disadvantage have eroded the moral sense of many young people. "It is as my father says," Absalom dutifully responds to Kumalo's prodding, but he cannot himself explain his own actions. And exactly why Absalom did what he did remains one of the "mysteries" to which there will be no answer.

Nevertheless, Absalom confesses, marries his girl to give the baby a name, and bears up under his fate. His two accomplices, egged on by the militant John, simply deny their involvement. They are completely exonerated owing to what the judge and his assessors deem insufficient proof, while Absalom is condemned to death. Some have taken Paton to be criticizing South African justice, so particular within the courtroom and so negligent without, but the author's accomplishment is that the reader can both understand the reasoning behind the guilty verdict and yet wince at the pronouncement of the sentence.

Ultimately, the humility, honesty, and persevering hope of Kumalo and his friends prove more fruitful than the corrosive anger and cynicism of John and the two thieves (who are involved in other criminal exploits). Good emerges from the wreck of the tragedy. Jarvis and Kumalo meet in a deeply moving but understated scene of shared and interlocking grief. Where Jarvis once saw only "a dirty old parson" from a "dirty old wood-and-iron church," he now sees a human being in anguish as great as his own. Jarvis's eyes open to his son's concerns for the blacks and he begins to help them where he can. He contributes to the boys' club, arranges for an agricultural consultant to help restore the ravaged earth of Ndotsheni, and determines to build a new church for Kumalo. For his part, Kumalo returns home with an expanded family, consisting of Gertrude's little son (Gertrude has mysteriously disappeared back into the big city) and his pregnant daughter-in-law. He also becomes more active, working with the agricultural consultant and encouraging the local chief to serve his people rather than indulge his arbitrary and trivial power over them.

The beauty of the language is part of the magic of *Cry, the Beloved Country*: the poetic Zulu speech, the cadences of the King James Bible, the mythic quality of much of the prose. Paton threads through sounds and images that make the story come alive: the gold of the mines that cause the devastation of the slums and the golden words of Msimangu's sermon that restore Kumalo's heart; the raucous, irresponsible laughter in the black townships; the cacophony of white voices addressing the "native problem" (vaguely reminiscent of the empty discourse in the pub in *The Waste Land*); the rush of the river when torrential rain stops. And the description of Kumalo's vigil the night before his son's execution is sublime.

After initial widespread adulation, critics began to find fault with *Cry, the Beloved Country*, seeing it as sentimental and propagandistic, more a treatise than a work of art. The novel tends to survive these objections, however, because the whole is greater than the sum of the parts. Wherever one probes a weak spot, the novel resists at some other point; as Lewis Gannett put it, it is "both unabashedly innocent and subtly sophisticated." The mythic narrative involving the search for the lost son blends with a realistic picture of a modern society. The novel's earnest idealism is offset by the amorphous sense of fear that pervades the country and by the suppressed fury the characters carry within them. Kumalo and Msimangu can erupt in anger and yield to subtle cruelty, and the brows of the young official at Diepkloof are constantly knitted against the difficulty of his work. (Paton's own increasingly tight-lipped expression was his response to the frustrations he faced.)

Where *Cry, the Beloved Country* grows too fable-like it suddenly turns analytical; where too discursive, it waxes poetical. Edward Callan, Paton's chief critic, has done a thorough job of delineating Paton's techniques, but, at the same time, it is not necessary to overstate the novel's purely literary pretensions in order to appreciate its achievement. Dan Jacobson, the self-exiled South African novelist, put *Cry, the Beloved Country* above strictly literary, political, or moral considerations into a category of works he called "proverbial."

Behind much of the criticism of Paton's novel one can make out a political edge. Early objectors to the novel tended to be white South Africans who bridled at its grim portrayal of black life. When the first film version was shown, the wife of the nationalist Afrikaner politician D. F. Malan remarked, "Surely, Mr. Paton, you don't really think things are like that?" The novel was not permitted in the schools until a few years before Paton's death. Later objections came from black militants and their sympathizers, who saw the novel as an expression of white liberalism and mocked Paton's belief in boys' clubs, for example. But the author was not so shallow as to imagine that boys' clubs *per se* were the ultimate solution to South Africa's dilemma. Paton makes clear in the novel that the renewed ameliorative efforts in the aftermath of the tragedy are a good beginning: but "when that dawn will come, of our emancipation, from the fear of bondage and the bondage of fear, why, that is a secret."

Nevertheless, Paton was modest enough to appreciate the good such measures could do. Paton personally paid for the education of countless black youngsters, gave financial help to many others who were in need, and contributed enormous amounts of time and money to his church, to charitable organizations, and to institutes working for social improvement. These commitments expressed his larger conviction that, as he said elsewhere, "the only power which can resist the power of fear is the power of love"—that the only way to achieve justice in South Africa was through a change in the hearts of enough people to make a difference. The militants who faulted Paton for proposing "love" as a solution to social and political injustice did not seem to realize how much of the groundwork for their political activism had been prepared through voluntary organizations of the kind Paton labored in and supported.

So, too, with the novel itself. Noting the blows it took from later militants, the black South African novelist Richard Rive defended *Cry, the Beloved Country*, calling it a "watershed" in South African fiction in that it brought the racial question into literary purview and widely influenced later writers. The Angolan writer Sousa Jamba read the novel at age fifteen in a second-hand copy that smelled of kerosene because, he surmised, its previous owners had stayed up nights to read it. Jamba carried it with him everywhere, and "forgot that what I was reading was written by a white man."

Even disdainful black writers such as the South African poet Dennis Brutus had to admit the novel's power and influence. And while deploring much in the characterizations, Ezekiel Mphahlele, another South African writer, concedes that *Cry, the Beloved Country* is "the first work in the history of South African fiction in which the black man looms so large." Although he did not like the portrait of the humble Zulu priest (preferring the angry John Kumalo instead), Mphahlele implicitly admits that it was true to life.

In Stephen Kumalo, Paton has painted a full picture of an African man, a good but flawed human being, complete with an inner life and a moral compass. The judge's sophisticated legal reasoning in no way surpasses the rural parson's own horrified grasp of his son's murderous act. Furthermore, Paton portrays his black characters in the dignity of individual responsibility even as he shows the restricted circumstances in which they must maneuver.

Paton's preoccupation with individual responsibility must partly have been derived from his experience at the Diepkloof Reformatory, where he stressed education, introduced extensive vocational training, and made many improvements in diet, clothing, sanitation, and living conditions. He became famous for successfully putting into practice the theories of experts in juvenile delinquency who believed that freedom could be used as an instrument of reform and rehabilitation.

Paton canceled many of the harsh and restrictive rules that had been in operation before his tenure, and the results were gratifying. The rate of escapes plunged sharply. After a rocky start, his furlough and home-leave program was an astonishing success. Thousands and thousands of boys took their respective leaves and returned with no trouble; very few absconded. Alas, one furloughed boy did commit a serious crime, breaking into a white woman's home and murdering her. He became the basis for the character Absalom Kumalo.

In some ways what Paton achieved at Diepkloof was the fulfillment of a liberal dream, epitomized when he had the high barbed wire gates of the compound torn down and replaced with ... flower beds! The freer the boys were, the less subject to punitive rules, the better they behaved, and the less likely they were to escape. But this behavior was not achieved through the simpleminded "compassion" in currency today. It developed within a framework of authority through which Paton labored to develop his charges' capacity for internal control. He employed military-style discipline in the work details and had the boys march and drill in parades conducted by his capable Afrikaner assistants, who were themselves in a civilian wing of the military service during the depression and war. Surprisingly or unsurprisingly, depending on one's point of view, these parades were relished by the boys, who took great pride in them.

Paton instituted daily Bible lessons and encouraged evening hymn singing, often conducted by his one black assistant or by Paton himself. He gradually built up his pupils' self-discipline by exposing them to the temptations they would face on the outside, and he granted them more and more freedom as they showed themselves more and more capable of handling it. He kept careful files on all of them and exercised great care in choosing them for furloughs. Furthermore, he sealed their behavior through pledges of responsibility. In solemn ceremonies, the boys made promises of trust and Paton issued badges of honor. Two boys who absconded while on separate furloughs eventually turned themselves in to the local police;

when asked by the police why they had turned themselves in, both replied that it was because of their "promise."

The point is that while Paton did believe that the "root causes" of black crime lay in conditions in South Africa, for which whites were largely responsible, he also knew what painstaking care, what investment of self, and what demands on the individual black person were involved in undoing the effects of these causes. He knew that even his best efforts did not always succeed; with all the good he was able to accomplish at Diepkloof, he was never able to eliminate corporal punishment entirely. All this gave him a kind of clear-eyed wisdom that served him well in his activities after 1948.

MARK HESTENES ON GRAHAM GREENE AND ALAN PATON

Two modern novelists who have made a contribution to both the literary world and the world of religious thought are the recently deceased writers, Graham Greene (1904–1991) and Alan Paton (1903–1988). Both writers have explored the mysteries of faith through the art of literature.

In 1940 Greene produced what many critics regard as his finest work, *The Power and the Glory*.[2] Greene developed his masterpiece against the inhospitable background of the severe religious persecutions in Mexico during the 1930s. In 1948 Paton's book, *Cry, the Beloved Country*[3] was published. The novel remains a best seller to the present day and 'continues to sell a six figure total every year'.[4] Both novels are written against situations of crises and address many parallel issues in two different parts of the world. Both attempt to portray God and faith in a harsh, demanding and desolate world. As will become apparent in this article, it is my view that neither Mexico nor South Africa are definite geographic locations in the minds of these authors. Rather, both have important universal significance. (...)

The Wasteland—Erosion, Barrenness and Dacay

Eliot's *The Waste Land* is a static, atrophied world of spiritual inertia and moral desolation. His poem portrays a decaying world and a barren landscape.[14] We read:

Dead mountain mouth of carious teeth that cannot spit
Here one can neither stand nor lie nor sit
There is not even silence in the mountains
But dry sterile thunder without rain
There is not even solitude in the mountains
But red sullen faces sneer and snarl
From doors of mudcracked houses ... [15]

In the opening chapters of *The Power and the Glory* and *Cry, the Beloved Country*, we encounter a similarly seedy and decaying world. It is a world of erosion of land and people. Both Greene and Paton feel compassion for this land, as well as the people about whom they write. (...)

The opening lines of *Cry, the Beloved Country* are both disturbing and uplifting. We hear of the lovely road that leads from Ixopo into the hills and of Paton's great respect for the close affinity between people and the land. We hear of the author's pleas for mankind to protect the land as part of God's unique creation. Unfortunately, the ground is being decimated. The hills that look so watered and luscious hide the erosion of the valleys. The constant erosion will soon endanger all the people in the area. He describes the impact of erosion and decay in the following majestic words: 'The great hills stand desolate and the earth is torn away like flesh. The lightning flashes over them, the clouds pour down upon them, the dead streams come to life, full of the red blood of the earth. Down in the valleys women scratch the soil that is left and the maize hardly reaches the height of a man. They are valleys of old men and old women, of mothers and children. The men are away, the young men and women are away. The soil cannot hold them anymore.'[18] In this opening prophetic scene, Paton describes the soft underbelly of South African society. He describes the plight of the nation as being that of desolation.

The Mexican and South African People—Spiritual, Moral and Social Decay

In Greene's book, the themes of desolation and decay lead to a sense of illness throughout the whole land. It is an illness that stretches from the damp river port through the swampy interior to the mountain country. It is a sick and dying land. (...)

In *Cry, the Beloved Country*, the social decay of the countryside is also experienced in the city. The leading character, Father Kumalo, comes to Johannesburg; where he hears about the afflictions of the city: 'So they all talked about the sickness of the land, of the broken tribe and the broken house, of young men and young; women that went away and forgot their customs, and lived loose and idle lives.'[21] In the author's opinion, the reason for this social and moral decay is the devastating impact of Western culture on African society and the resultant breakdown of the tribal heritage and home and family life.

The white people insulate themselves behind their power and affluence in order to blind themselves to what is going on. Hence we read: 'Gold, gold, gold. The country is going to be rich again. Shares are up from twenty shillings to a hundred shillings, think of it, thank God for it.... It would be nice to have paid more to the miners. Well anyone can see that this is muddled, because the price of shares has really nothing to do with the question of wages at all, for this is a matter determined solely by mining costs and the price of gold.'[22] The whites plead ignorance of the causes of crime and pay poor wages and see no link between their prosperity and the poverty and crime around them.

The author's white hero, Jarvis, links this depressing social and moral situation with a disastrous view of

Christianity. He writes, 'The truth is that our Christian civilisation is riddled through and through with dilemma. We believe in the brotherhood of man, but we do not want it in South Africa. We believe that God endows men with diverse gifts, and that human life depends for its fullness on their employment and enjoyment, but we are afraid to explore this belief too deeply. We believe in help for the underdog, but we want him to stay under.'[23] The portrait then is one of destruction and decadence. It is a land of violence, crime and fear, ruled by fear.

The Spiritual Quest of the Whisky Priest and Kumato

A major theme of Eliot's poem is the salvation of the wasteland. The poem explores the possibility of the moral and spiritual and intellectual restoration of the wasteland.[24] The quest for spiritual and moral truth is, however, hazardous and includes severe trials. The place of testing is a stark, barren and fearful location. Hence we read:

> In this decayed hole among the mountains
> In the faint moonlight, the grass is singing
> Over the tumbled graves, about the chapel
> There is the empty chapel, only the wind's home.
> It has no windows, and the door swings,
> Dry bones can harm no one.[25]

The kingdom of God has both current and eschatological significance. God's reign takes place particularly through the church and her people. God's purpose is to transform this world and to make Christians uneasy 'with anything less than God's righteousness, justice and peace in the world'.[26] In this article I will reflect on the reign of God as witnessed through the humble discipleship of the whisky priest and Kumalo. The whisky priest and Kumalo are God's confused and humble servants who become instruments of God's love and compassion (especially Kumalo) or an instrument of God's sacrificial purpose (the whisky priest).

It is fruitful to highlight the whisky priest's and Kumalo's spiritual quest as proceeding through four stages. These correspond to four of the main stages found in mystical development. The stages are: The Awakening of the Self; The Purification of the Self; The Dark Night of the Soul; The Illumination of the Self.[27]

A. *The Awakening of the Self*

First in the course of mystical stages is the pivotal event of the awakening of the self. This awakening resembles what many religious writers call 'conversion'. One writer asserts:

> Conversion is primarily an unselfing. The first birth of the individual is into his own little world ... Conversion then is the larger world consciousness now pressing in on the individual consciousness. Often it breaks in suddenly and becomes a great new revelation.[28]

(...)

The awakening of the self also comes for Kumalo through the experience of pain and suffering. At the start of the novel, Kumalo receives a letter from Johannesburg. Johannesburg is a place where people from the country go and do not return from again. The letter tells him of the mysterious sickness of his sister. He has to choose between going to Johannesburg, or ignoring the letter. He chooses to go in order to save his sister. We read: 'The journey had begun. And now the fear back again, the fear of the unknown, the fear of the great city where boys were killed crossing the streets, the fear of Gertrude's sickness. Deep down the fear for his son. Deep down the fear of a man who lives in a world not made for him, whose own world is slipping away, dying, being destroyed, beyond any recall.'[29]

B. *The Purification of the Self*

After the awakening of the self, the self is set on a new path. Activity is now the watchword and pilgrimage becomes the chief purpose of life. It is also a time of character formation.

The purifying of the self is imperative in order that the warped views of reality be overcome. The awakened self is plunged into a new world. (...)

In *Cry, the Beloved Country*, Kumalo's first encounter with Johannesburg is a painful experience. A fellow traveller robs him, but another man helps him to find his way to the Mission House in Sophiatown. Here he begins to encounter the harshness of city life. He discovers that his sister has become an illegal liquor seller and a prostitute. In his first meeting with her, Kumalo delivers a stern word of rebuke: 'You have shamed us.... A liquor seller, a prostitute, with a child.... Your brother a priest.'[32] To his surprise, through his confused ministry her regeneration begins. After only one day in the city, Kumalo has the satisfaction of seeing his sister and child reunited with him.

C. *The Dark Night of the Soul*

Following a period of awakening and purging, a dark night of the soul is usually experienced. Exhaustion sets in with a devastating sense of blankness and stagnation. The state of anguish is associated with an experience of the absence of God. (...)

Kumalo goes through a [...] dark night of the soul in the search for his son. His recovery of his sister is a prelude to the search for his son. His prolonged journey through the sordid Johannesburg underworld leads to a crisis of faith. His quest ends in bitterness when he finds his son in prison for killing a white man. We read: 'My child, my child —Yes, my father, — At last I have found you —Yes my father —And it is too late.'[35] One of his fellow priests remarks, 'There are times no doubt when God seems no more to be about the world.'[36]

D. *The Illumination of the Self*

After the dark night of the soul, there is a decisive turn back into the light of self-awareness. It is the result of the painful purging of the human spirit. The consequence of this process is a new resolve about God and adjustments to new norms and standards. (...)

The motif of illumination also penetrates this part of Kumalo's existence. Kumalo returns to Ixopo a changed person. He has been transformed by deep personal suffering. Through his tortured journey, Kumalo had come to see the kingdom of God. He is now a more stoical person who is willing to bear the suffering of others. He is now willing to take the initiative and make important choices for himself and others. He begins to organise the white and black communities to join together in their fight to restore their land. The journey ends with a message of hope and doubt.

Kumalo's final illumination comes at the end of the novel. In the last pages, he makes a trip to a nearby mountain. The mountain is a place where he goes when facing crucial decisions of his life. Here he shares his son's anguish on the morning of his hanging. His consolation comes from God and knowing that his fellow priests are together with his son. Hence we conclude with these magnificent words: 'And when he expected it, he rose to his feet and took off his hat and laid it down on the earth and clasped his hands before him. And while he stood there the sun rose in the east.'[38]

To See the Kingdom

Throughout both novels the pervasive presence of God is evident as witnessed through the humble discipleship of the two chief characters and several named and nameless supporting figures. Both novels are pregnant with implications concerning the transcendence and immanence of God.

Greene's novel is usually portrayed as an example of God as pursuer or hunter. The theme of Francis Thompson's poem, *The Hound of Heaven*, is quoted to illustrate this theme. In later life, Greene has continued to stress that he feels that God is still pursuing or hounding him.[39] Paton's novel could also be interpreted in this light. Kumalo is God's reluctant disciple and yet he is used as an instrument of love, peace and redemption.

Paton has, however, also associated this poem with the ruthless pursuit of people by the Oxford Group (Moral Rearmament) and the South African Security Police.[40] (...)

Paton's understanding of the invisible God has much in common with that of Greene. Paton has indicated that he has difficulty understanding the doctrine of the Trinity, and yet he has developed a subtle and appealing vision of God. In the opening scene of his novel, we sense that Paton believes in a God who affirms the goodness of creation and the potential goodness of people. Paton has often remarked upon his belief that he desires to be an instrument of the good, which for him means being an instrument of God. He has described God as being all powerful and concerned with attracting believers to cooperate with His will. The church is called to bring comfort in a desolate world through being God's instruments of peace and His good power.[44] Finally, for Paton, faith, hope and love are all grounded in the belief that God reigns and that God is good.

Notes

2. G. Greene, *The Power and the Glory* (London: Penguin, 1982). All passages from the novel quoted in this article are from this edition.

3. A. Paton, *Cry, the Beloved Country* (London: Penguin, 1984). All passages from the novel quoted in this article are from this edition.

4. E. Callan, *Alan Paton* (Boston: Twayne, 1982) p. 1.

14. B. Southam, *A Student's Guide to the Selected Poems of T.S. Eliot.* (London: Faber, 1981) p. 81.

15. T.S. Eliot, *Collected Poems* (London: Faber, 1959) p. 74. Lines 339–45.

18. *Cry, the Beloved Country*, p. 7. Stephen Gray has commented suggestively about the relationship between land and people in South African fiction. He writes: 'Landscape, in South African realist fiction, never merely sustains and magnifies man; it dwarfs and overwhelms, it remains unyielding and destructive.' Refer to Stephen Gray, *Southern African Literature: An Introduction* (Cape Town: David Philips, 1979), p. 151. In my view, this is only partly true of Paton's books.

21. *Cry, the Beloved Country*, p. 22.

22. *Cry, the Beloved Country*, p. 147.

23. *Cry, the Beloved Country*, p. 134.

24. *A Student's Guide to the Selected Poems of T.S. Eliot*, p. 76.

25. *Collected Poems*, p. 76. Lines 685–90.

26. J. De Gruchy, *The Church Struggle in South Africa*, 2nd edn (Cape Town: David Philips, 1989) p. 199.

27. I am grateful to my colleague, L. Hodne, for this original insight regarding Kumalo's spiritual development. I have expanded on her insight in a number of ways, including making a comparison between the whisky priest and Kumalo.

28. E. Underhill, *Mysticism* (New York: Meridian, 1955) p. 176. The sections following the sub-headings are paraphrases from her book. I have followed L. Hodne's revised order of the stages.

29. *Cry, the Beloved Country*, p. 15.

32. *Cry, the Beloved Country*, p. 29.

35. *Cry, the Beloved Country*, p. 87.

36. *Cry, the Beloved Country*, p. 67.

38. *Cry,the Beloved Country*, p. 236.

39. N. Sherry, *The Life of Graham Greene Vol 1: 1904-1939* (New York: Viking Press1989) p. xxii.

40. A. Paton, *Towards the Mountain* (New York: Scribners, 1977) p. 121.

44. K. Smith, "Influence of Religious Traditions on the Life of Alan Paton", M.Th. dissertation, University of South Africa, Pretoria, 1987, p. 91.

Works by Alan Paton

Cry, the Beloved Country, 1948.

Too Late the Phalarope, 1953.

The Land and People of South Africa, 1955.

South Africa in Transition, 1956.

Hope for South Africa, 1958.

The People Wept, 1958.

The Last Journey, 1959.

Debbie Go Home, 1961.

Tales from a Troubled Land, 1961.

Hofmeyr, 1964.

Sponono, 1964.

Instrument of Thy Peace, 1968.

The Long View, ed. Edward Callan, 1968.

Kontakion for You Departed, 1969.

Apartheid and the Archbishop, 1973.

Knocking on the Door, ed. Colin Gardner, 1975.

Towards the Mountain, 1980.

Ah, But Your Land Is Beautiful, 1981.

Journey Continued, 1988 (posthumous).

Annotated Bibliography

Asein, Samuel O. "Christian Moralism and Apartheid: Paton's *Cry the Beloved Country* Reassessed." *Africa Quarterly* 14, nos. 1–2 (1974), pp. 53–63.

Examines the fundamental religious philosophy guiding Paton's social vision.

Callan, Edward. Cry, the Beloved Country: *A Novel of South Africa*. Twayne's Masterwork Studies. Boston: G.K. Hall & Co., 1991. 129 p.

A thorough examination of characters, themes, language, and style by one of the foremost Paton scholars.

Folley, Andrew. "'Considered as a Social Record': A Reassessment of *Cry, the Beloved Country*." *English in Africa* 25, no. 2 (October 1998), pp. 63–92.

A critical exploration of the novel both as a work of literature and as a historical record and representation of South African society.

Hogan, Patrick Colm. "Paternalism, Ideology, and Ideological Critique: Teaching *Cry, the Beloved Country*." *College Literature* 19–2, nos. 3–1 (October 1992–February 1993), pp. 206–10.

Examines *Cry, the Beloved Country* as a postcolonial novel with a pedagogical approach to the problems of race relations.

Holland, R.W.H. "Fiction and History: Fact and Invention in Alan Paton's Novel *Cry, the Beloved Country*." *Zambezia: The Journal of the University of Rhodesia* 5, no. 2 (1977), pp. 129–39.

Examines how Paton weaves history and invention together to form the plot and emphasize the themes of *Cry, the Beloved Country*.

Mbeboh, K.W. "*Cry, the Beloved Country:* A Liberal Apology." *Cameroon Studies in English & French* 1 (1976), pp. 71–77.

Argues that *Cry, the Beloved Country* expresses a "white liberal" understanding of the situation of South African blacks.

Medalie, David. "'A Corridor Shut at Both Ends': Admonition and Impasse in Van der Post's *In A Province* and Paton's *Cry, the Beloved Country.*" *English in Africa* 25, no. 2 (October 1998), pp. 93–110.

Considers both novels in terms of the problems posed by urbanization of traditionally agrarian societies.

Monye, A.A. "*Cry, the Beloved Country*: Should We Merely Cry? *Nigeria Magazine*, 144 (1983), pp. 74–83.

Offers a critical analysis of the political ideology of the novel.

Morphet, Tony. "Stranger Fictions: Trajectories in the Liberal Novel." *World Literature Today: A Literary Quarterly of the University of Oklahoma* 70, no. 1 (Winter 1996), pp. 53–58.

Compares Nadine Gordimer's treatment of the "stranger," and such a character's relation to modernity in *A World of Strangers* with the way that theme is handled by J.M. Coetzee and by Paton in *Cry, the Beloved Country.*

Ndlovu, Victor and Alet Kruger. "Translating English Terms of Address in *Cry, the Beloved Country* into Zulu." *South African Journal of African Languages/Suid-Afrikaanse Tydskrif vir Afrikatale* 18, no. 2 (May1998), pp. 50–56.

Examines how *Cry, the Beloved Country* has been translated into Zulu.

Odumuh, Emmanuel. "The Theme of Love in Alan Paton's *Cry, the Beloved Country.*" *Kuka: Journal of Creative and Critical Writing* (1980–1981), pp. 41–50.

Explores Paton's belief in the importance of love, as presented in the novel, for the establishment of a good and just society.

Oosthuizen, Michèle. "Teaching South African Literature." *CRUX: A Journal on the Teaching of English* 20, no. 3 (August 1986), pp. 39–44.

Explores ways of teaching *Cry, the Beloved Country* and Athol Fugard's Boesman and Lena.

Rive, Richard. "The Liberal Tradition in South African Literature." *Contrast: South African Literary Journal* 14, no. 3 (July 1983), pp. 19–31.

Compares *Cry, the Beloved Country* with Peter Abrahams' *Path of Thunder* regarding the values the authors espouse.

Sharma, R. C. "Alan Paton's *Cry, the Beloved Country*: The Parable of Compassion." *Literary Half-Yearly* 19, no. 2 (1978), pp. 64–82.

Explores the responses to suffering presented in Paton's novel.

Smock, Susan Wanles. "*Lost in the Stars* and *Cry, the Beloved Country*: A Thematic Comparison." *North Dakota Quarterly* 48, no. 3 (1980), pp. 53–59.

Examines the changes Maxwell Anderson made to Paton's novel for the musical and how they influence the thematic material.

Watson, Stephen. "*Cry, the Beloved Country* and the Failure of Liberal Vision." *English in Africa* 9, no. 1 (May 1982), pp. 29–44.

Analyzes Paton's liberalism as it is expressed by the novel.

Contributors

Harold Bloom is Sterling Professor of the Humanities at Yale University and Henry W. and Albert A. Berg Professor of English at the New York University Graduate School. He is the author of over 20 books, including *Shelley's Mythmaking* (1959), *The Visionary Company* (1961), *Blake's Apocalypse* (1963), *Yeats* (1970), *A Map of Misreading* (1975), *Kabbalah and Criticism* (1975), *Agon: Toward a Theory of Revisionism* (1982), *The American Religion* (1992), *The Western Canon* (1994), and *Omens of Millennium: The Gnosis of Angels, Dreams, and Resurrection* (1996). *The Anxiety of Influence* (1973) sets forth Professor Bloom's provocative theory of the literary relationships between the great writers and their predecessors. His most recent books include *Shakespeare: The Invention of the Human* (1998), a 1998 National Book Award finalist, *How to Read and Why* (2000), *Genius: A Mosaic of One Hundred Exemplary Creative Minds* (2002), and *Hamlet: Poem Unlimited* (2003). In 1999, Professor Bloom received the prestigious American Academy of Arts and Letters Gold Medal for Criticism, and in 2002 he received the Catalonia International Prize.

Horton Davies was Professor of Divinity at Rhodes University in South Africa and Professor of the History of Christianity at Princeton. He has published extensively on religion.

Sheridan Baker was the author of books on Henry Fielding, Ernest Hemingway, and Alan Paton. He also wrote *The Practical Stylist*, a handbook for teaching writing.

Edmund Fuller was a novelist, critic and social historian.

Martin Tucker edited *Modern British Literature* in the "Library of Literary Criticism" series and taught English at Long Island University.

Myron Matlaw is the author of the college writing textbook *Pro and Con*, has written extensively on early American theater, and has taught English at Queens College of the City University of New York.

Robert L. Duncan was a Professor of English at Illinois State University.

Novelist, essayist, and winner of the Booker Prize in 1983, **J.M. Coetzee** is a member of the Committee on Social Thought at the University of Chicago and a Research Fellow at the University of Adelaide. His most recent book is *Youth: Scenes from Provincial Life II*.

Tony Adler is a theater critic and arts writer, and a founder of The Actors Gymnasium.

Carol Iannone teaches in the Gallatin School of Individualized Study at New York University and has published essays in *Commentary*, *The New Criterion*, *Antioch Review*, and *Modern Age*.

Mark Hestenes teaches in the Department of Practical Theology at the University of South Africa.

Acknowledgments

"Alan Paton: Literary Artist and Anglican" by Horton Davies. From *The Hibbert Journal: A Quarterly of Religion, Theology, and Philosophy* L (October 1951–July 1952): 265–268. © 1952 by George Allen & Unwin Ltd. Reprinted by permission.

"Paton's Beloved Country and the Morality of Geography" by Sheridan Baker. From *College English* 19, no. 2 (November 1957): 56–61. © 1957 by the National Council of Teachers of English. Reprinted by permission.

"Alan Paton: Tragedy and Beyond" by Edmund Fuller. From *Books with Men Behind Them* by Edmund Fuller. New York: Random House, 1959: 94–99. © 1959, 1961, 1962 by Edmund Fuller. Reprinted by permission.

"The Color of South African Literature" by Martin Tucker. From *Africa in Modern Literature: A Survey of Contemporary Writing in English*. New York: Fredrick Ungar Publishing Co., 1967: 223–225. © 1967 by Frederick Ungar Publishing Co., Inc. Reprinted by permission.

"Alan Paton's *Cry, the Beloved Country* and Maxwell Anderson's/ Kurt Weill's *Lost in the Stars*: A Consideration of Genres" by Myron Matlaw. From *Arcadia: Zeitschrift für Vergleichende Literaturwissenschaft* 10, no. 3 (1975): 262–266. © 1975 by Walter de Gruyter & Co. Reprinted by permission.

"The Suffering Servant in Novels by Paton, Bernanos, and Schwarz-Bart" by Robert L. Duncan. From *Christian Scholar's Review* 16, no. 2 (January 1987): 122–128. © 1987 by Robert L. Duncan. Reprinted by permission.

"Simple Language, Simple People: Smith, Paton, Mikro" by J.M. Coetzee. From *White Writing: On the Culture of Letters*

Index